Also by Neil Thompson:

Stress Matters
Tackling Bullying and Harassment in the Workplace
Loss and Grief: A Guide for Human Services Practitioners* (ed.)
Promoting Equality: Challenging Discrimination and Oppression
    (second edition)*
People Skills (second edition)*
Communication and Language*
Understanding Social Work: Preparing for Practice (second
    edition)*
Anti-Discriminatory Practice (fourth edition)*

* Also published by Palgrave

People Problems

NEIL THOMPSON

CONSULTANT EDITOR: JO CAMPLING

First published 2006 by
PALGRAVE MACMILLAN
Houndmills, Basingstoke, Hampshire RG21 6XS and
175 Fifth Avenue, New York, N.Y. 10010
Companies and representatives throughout the world

PALGRAVE MACMILLAN is the global academic imprint of the Palgrave Macmillan division of St. Martin's Press, LLC and of Palgrave Macmillan Ltd. Macmillan® is a registered trademark in the United States, United Kingdom and other countries. Palgrave is a registered trademark in the European Union and other countries.

ISBN-13: 978–1–4039–4304–0
ISBN 10: 1–4039–4304–4

This book is printed on paper suitable for recycling and made from fully managed and sustained forest sources.

A catalogue record for this book is available from the British Library.

A catalog record for this book is available from the Library of Congress.

10   9   8   7   6   5   4   3   2   1
15   14 13 12 11 10 09 08 07 06

Printed in China

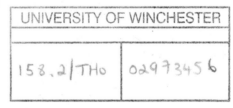

For Bernard

Contents

CONTENTS

The author

Neil Thompson has the best part of thirty years' experience in social work as a practitioner, manager, educator, author, editor and consultant. He was formerly Professor of Applied Social Studies at Staffordshire University and has also served as a Visiting Professor at the University of Liverpool and North East Wales Institute (University of Wales). He now works as an independent trainer and consultant with Avenue Consulting Ltd, a company he established in 2000 (www.avenueconsulting.co.uk). He was also responsible for setting up the *humansolutions* self-help website (www.humansolutions.org.uk), dealing with 'workplace well-being' issues.

Neil has over 100 publications to his name, including best-selling books, papers in learned journals and training and open learning materials. He was the founding editor of the *British Journal of Occupational Learning* (www.traininginstitute.co.uk) and has been involved with a number of other journals. He is the series editor for the *Theory into Practice* series of books published by Russell House Publishing.

Neil has qualifications in social work; management; training and development; and mediation and alternative dispute resolution, as well as a first-class honours degree and a PhD.

Neil has been a speaker at conferences in the UK, Ireland, Greece, Spain, Norway, the Netherlands, Hong Kong, Canada, the United States and Australia. He is a Chartered Fellow of the Chartered Institute of Personnel and Development and a fellow of the Institute of Training and Occupational Learning. In addition, he was elected as a Fellow of the Royal Society of Arts for his contribution to workplace learning.

His website address is: www.neilthompson.info.

Preface

This book has arisen as a result of the success of my earlier work, *People Skills* (Thompson, 2002a). The aim of the earlier book was to provide an introduction to a range of skills involved in what can broadly be described as 'people work'. By this I mean the type of work that involves dealing with people and their problems in a variety of settings. I am pleased to say that I have had extensive positive feedback about *People Skills*. It has been described as an excellent introduction to the broad repertoire of skills that people need in working with other people. While that book concentrated on the skills involved and the underpinning knowledge required for practising such skills, it is now recognized that a further work is needed which concentrates on specific techniques or tools of the trade. This book should then be seen as a complementary volume accompanying *People Skills* – a sort of companion volume.

The term, 'people work', is perhaps one that is used by different people in different ways. It is therefore important to be clear about who this book is designed to help. My own interpretation of the term 'people skills' is a very broad one. It incorporates any form of work or interaction which is based on trying to help people, whether individuals or groups, to address problems they encounter. This includes all forms of management because, when we are focusing on issues such as finances, structures and systems, we are always doing so through the medium of the people who are employed by that organization. As the saying goes, an organization's most important resource is its human resource – its people. In recent years, we have seen a shift towards 'managerialism', with its strong emphasis on targets and performance indicators, with the increased risk that the people dimension gets overlooked or at least goes out of focus as more technical matters take centre stage. This book, then, will be of relevance and value to managers across a wide range of organizational settings and functions.

This book should also be of value and benefit to people working in the caring professions, those particular disciplines which have as their focus particular problems, demands and challenges. This would include social work and social care, nursing and other health-related professions, counselling, advice work, youth and community work, and so on. Indeed, it is a hallmark of the caring professions that they are concerned with the problems of health, welfare and so on that people encounter in their daily lives in certain circumstances. However, this does not exhaust our list of groups of people who may find points of interest and value here. We should also consider other groups who can come under the broad umbrella term of 'human services'. This would include staff involved in education and training, people involved in police and criminal justice work and, indeed, people involved in local government and related work that involves dealing with the general public or specific sectors of the local community. This, then, is a book that has broad application.

Despite this breadth, one thing that all these different groups of potential readers have in common is an emphasis on human needs. This common theme of attempting to meet human needs is something that acts as a binding theme of a book – it unifies many elements of the issues discussed. By and large, attempting to meet human needs involves addressing the problems that stand in the way of those needs being met by other means. In other words, dealing with human needs is about problem solving, the focus of this book.

This is a huge topic, and clearly one book will not be able to provide all that there is to know about this vast subject matter. However, I do hope that it will provide enough and give you a good grounding in the range of issues that need to be considered and provide you with some practical tools on which you can build your professional practice as a 'people worker'.

NEIL THOMPSON

Acknowledgements

I am very grateful to a number of people for offering constructive comments on an earlier draft of the work, namely: Duncan Pritchard, Principal of Aran Hall School; Graham Thompson, University of Wales, Bangor; Bernard Moss and Mark Savage, Staffordshire University; John Bates, North East Wales Institute and Rob Kennett, Kent Constabulary.

My debt to Susan Thompson continues to be a significant one, and once again the finished product of the book has been improved by her contribution at a number of levels and a number of ways.

Margaret Holloway's excellent typing skills have also made an important contribution to the book and I am grateful to her for that.

Judy Marshall once again did an excellent job in preparing the typescript for publication. It is good to have such talented support.

Jo Campling again deserves considerable credit for the positive contribution she has made as consultant editor, guide and friend. I am also grateful for the invaluable support of Beverley Tarquini, Catherine Gray and Sheree Keep at the publishers.

Introduction

Working in the 'people professions' can be a source of great satisfaction and enjoyment. However, it is no exaggeration to state
that, where there are people, there are problems. Indeed, it would
be very naïve to assume that you could bring large numbers of
people together in workplaces or in society more broadly without
there being difficulties of some description. However, this is not a
reason for pessimism or negativity. Rather, it is an acceptance of
the challenge that, when we work with people, we need to have
well-developed problem-solving skills. Putting those skills to good
use can be an excellent source of satisfaction and pleasure in their
own right. Adopting a position of realism means that we have to
avoid the unhelpful extremes of, on the one hand, a destructive
pessimism that sees no hope and, on the other, a naïve optimism
that sees the world through rose-tinted spectacles. The reality is
that working with people has very many positives, but there will
inevitably be problems as well. A key aim of this book is to help
equip you to turn some of those problems into successes and
sources of satisfaction by helping you to develop the skills and
strategies that can play such an important role in working with
people and their problems.

The book is divided into three main parts: Part One can be seen
as an extended essay on what is involved in problem solving. This
entails looking at some key issues that can help us to understand
some of the complexities involved. In effect, Part One fulfils two
roles: on the one hand, it provides an introductory, scene-setting
overview in preparation for Part Two of the book. On the other
hand, it also provides an important analysis in its own right of
the knowledge, skills and values involved in problem solving in a
variety of settings. Part Two of the book presents fifty methods,
techniques or tools. Some of these are new to this volume; others
not so new. The aim is not to provide detailed step-by-step

instructions for you to follow, as that would be a gross oversimplification of the complexities involved in this demanding, but rewarding type of work. Rather, the idea of tools is that they provide a bridge between theory and practice. Tools will not do the job for you, but they will give you a framework to work to, to enable you to draw on the wisdom to be gleaned from the research and other people's experience in this area – so that you do not have to start from scratch with only your own experience to rely on. Part Two should help you to incorporate your own experience with the knowledge and understanding that we have gained from a long history of working with people and their problems. Each method or technique is explained so that you can develop an understanding of what is involved, in what circumstances it could possibly be used and with what objectives in mind. The ideas presented will not, of course, guarantee success in any particular venture but, if used appropriately, should increase the chances of a positive outcome.

Part Three is a shorter section comprising the guide to further learning. It includes references to further reading where appropriate, plus details of relevant websites where suitable ones exist.

There is a focus throughout the book on 'use of self'. What this means is that the tools are of no use on their own and can, in fact, be dangerous if not used properly. We need to draw on our own personal resources (knowledge, skills and values) to be able to put these tools to good use. Having a method or tool to draw upon does not give us an easy answer. In undertaking this type of work, we still need to draw on a good understanding of what makes people tick. We shall explore this point in more detail in Part One.

One important point to recognize is that some problems are not resolvable – that is, there are no guarantees that these tools or, indeed, any approach to a particular problem will be successful. This is important to note because, if we do not take this on board, we can, in effect, set ourselves up for stress. What I mean by this is that, if we set ourselves unrealistic targets, we create unrealistic expectations, something that is recognized as a significant source of stress (Thompson, 1999). Learning to be realistic about what can and cannot be achieved is an important part of professional development in people work. This is because we must avoid the disruptive extremes of: (i) being defeatist and cynical and assuming that progress cannot be made in circumstances where (with the right input from a skilled worker) progress may indeed be possible; and

(ii) as mentioned earlier, setting ourselves up for stress by having unrealistic expectations.

It is to be hoped that, in conjunction with the discussion of skills in *People Skills*, this book will help to equip you to tackle some of the very significant challenges that arise in working with people and their problems.

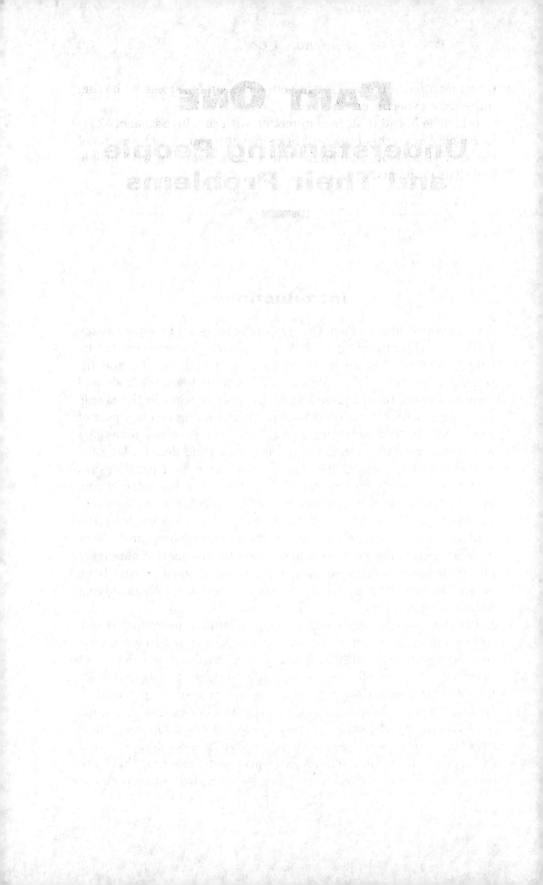

PART ONE

Understanding People and Their Problems

Introduction

As mentioned above, Part One of this book is an extended essay which has the aim of (i) providing a general introduction to the subject matter of problem solving in relation to people, and (ii) setting the scene for Part Two and the various tools, methods and techniques contained therein. Many people can work in the people professions without realizing that problem solving is a key part of what they do. For example, I have come across many managers who complain of people getting in the way of their doing their job – as if they fail to grasp that helping people solve their problems (so that they work to their maximum output) is a key part of any manager's role. Similarly, I have come across many social workers who get bogged down in 'providing services', who lose sight of the rationale for providing such services – that is, to solve a problem or meet a need. Many more examples could be provided of managers and professionals engaged in a wide range of settings who have fallen into the trap of failing to appreciate the problem-solving nature of their work.

For some people, problem solving is an explicit part of their role – for example, a community psychiatric nurse trying to work with somebody with mental health problems to avoid an eviction from their flat, or a debt advice worker trying to help a family to resolve financial problems that are spiralling out of control. For others, however, direct problem solving may not be a key part of their role, but problem-solving skills are required to enable them to do their bread and butter work. For example, a youth worker may be trying to develop a particular scheme or project, but finds that there are obstacles in the way of doing so (perhaps a conflict between two or more of the participants). Problem-solving skills will then need to be drawn upon, even though direct problem solving is not the object of the exercise. For people involved in management roles, both sides of this particular coin can be seen to apply – that is, a manager will have responsibility for certain areas of work and will, at times, need to adopt a problem-solving approach in order to achieve the particular objective. However, he or she is also quite free to become involved in problem-solving activities as a direct part of the managerial role – for example, in dealing with grievances, disciplinary matters and so on.

An important distinction to draw is that between people problems and problem people. By people problems, I mean the sort of difficulties and complications that arise when people come together – for example, conflict, stress, communication breakdowns. This is not to be confused with 'problem people'. Problem people is a term I prefer not to use because of its unhelpful connotations. It implies that somebody is 'by their very nature' difficult or a problem. This is a gross oversimplification of some very complex issues about how problems arise and how best they can be dealt with. To label individuals as problem people is to indulge in a judgemental attitude. This is a situation to be avoided because adopting a judgemental attitude means making a value judgement about an individual's worth and assuming that they are responsible for the problems concerned. There are a number of reasons why we should steer clear of this sort of reaction:

1. *It is often not fair* For example, someone may be labelled as lazy, but this is likely to mask underlying issues of motivation which are just as much a managerial responsibility as that of the individual (this is not to say that people are never lazy but, rather, that it is much more appropriate to try and find out why their motivation is so low rather than just write them off as a 'lazy person').
2. *It is rarely effective* Being judgemental simply does not help. It does not take us any further forward in our problem-solving activities and, in fact, can often act as a block to such activities.
3. *It can be counterproductive* Tensions and conflicts can be generated by adopting a judgemental attitude. Applying a negative label to somebody can actually, in some circumstances, encourage them to adopt the behaviour you are implicitly criticizing. For

example, labelling somebody as 'obstructive' may actually make that person less co-operative, rather than more.

4. *It fails to see the situation from the point of view of the person concerned*   I shall be arguing below that the important part of effective problem solving is the ability to put yourself in other people's shoes, to see the situation from their point of view. Being judgemental about somebody prevents us from doing this. If we fail to take account of the individual's point of view, then we are likely to generate resistance, rather than commitment, to making progress. This relates to the important concept of motivation, an issue that we shall explore in more detail below.

What is a problem?

Before going any further it is important to clarify what I mean by 'problems', given that the book is about problem-solving strategies. For the purposes of this book, a problem is anything that either brings about negatives (pain, suffering distress, anxiety and so on) or blocks positives (health, fulfilment, satisfaction, progress in achieving our goals and so on) or a mixture of the two. In a sense, having a problem can be defined as being in a situation that we want to get out of. Problem-solving methods are therefore tools we can use to help people get out of such situations.

Problems can come in all sorts of shapes and sizes and varying degrees of severity or intensity. They can reinforce one another and one can be the root cause of others – the issue of cause and effect is not a simple one. Sometimes problems can be manageable on their own, but in combination they can prove overwhelming. Problems are certainly not entirely subjective, but there is none the less an important subjective dimension. That is, if somebody perceives a situation as a problem, then it *is* a problem, in so far as that is how it will be experienced by the person(s) concerned – as a problem. As it was expressed quite some time ago now, 'the definition of the situation is real in its consequences' (Thomas and Znaniecki, 1958). For example, if someone is worried about something, even if this worry is unrealistic, it does not alter the fact that he or she is experiencing worry and thus has a problem (as defined above). It would be a serious mistake to disregard this problem by assuming that it is not a 'real' problem. If it is perceived as 'real', it will be experienced as 'real' and will therefore be 'real in its consequences'.

There is a close relationship between problems and unmet needs, and it is a two-way relationship. That is, unmet needs can cause problems and experiencing problems can lead to our needs not being met. An example of the former would be someone's need for affection leading to low self-esteem, while an example of the latter might be an aggressive manner leading to a need for affection not being met.

What is a 'people' problem?

As noted above, problems come in all shapes and sizes and can have different causes. They can be technical (the new software is incompatible with the existing software we use), financial (outgoings exceed income) or logistical (the equipment we need is not where we need it to be) and so on. While problems such as these will generally have human consequences (frustration, poverty or other such negative outcomes), what I refer to as 'people' problems have not only human consequences, but also human causes for the most part. This is primarily, but not exclusively, a question of relationships. Relationships can be wonderful and a great source of strength and joy. However, they can also be terrible and a source of great pain and problems. This can arise because of the nature of the relationship, a change in it or the ending of it.

Relationships are not only individual matters, of course. Problems arise because of relationships between groups or other 'factions' (genders, ethnic or religious groups and so on). We should therefore be wary of adopting too narrow a perspective on this.

Relationships involve a number of dimensions, but four in particular merit our attention here:

- *Power* We should be wary of seeing power as something an individual either has or does not have. Power is, by and large, a matter of relationships. For example, a manager may have power over an employee in the workplace, but that relationship may be reversed outside work if, for example, that employee is a special constable. Power is a very complex issue, but for present purposes we should note that it is an important dimension of relationships (and relationships are an important dimension of power).

- *Conflict* A common mistake is for people to assume that conflict is what occurs when relationships break down. However, in reality, relationships can be characterized by conflict over a very long period of time without ever breaking down. Conflict, or at least the potential for conflict, is present in all relationships.
- *Communication* Relationships exist through communication and are also a major channel of communication (consider, for example, how much of your communication is with people you are in some sort of relationship with, compared with communicating with people who are peripheral to your network of relationships).
- *Identity* Our sense of who we are arises, in part at least, from our relationships. For example, being a parent is not only a status, it is also a relationship. (In my own case, my identity as a parent stems from my relationship with my daughter.) Where there are problems in relationships, there can be problems of identity. Indeed, people experiencing major problems (a bereavement, for example) will often say: 'I don't know who I am anymore'.

Another important point to recognize about 'people' problems is that someone experiencing a problem can lead to other people experiencing problems. For example, someone who is having personal difficulties may, as a result of the build up of tension, indulge in bullying behaviour. Indeed, it is very commonly the case that someone *causing* problems is also *experiencing* problems. It is therefore important that we do not fall into the trap commonly known as 'the blame game'. Unacceptable behaviour is precisely that – unacceptable, but rather than simply condemning people for such behaviour, it can be far more fruitful (in both the short and long term) to look at why such behaviour is occurring and see whether action can be taken to change the underlying causes. This does not mean that people should not be held responsible for their actions – they certainly should – but, if we want to resolve problematic situations, then we need to go further (and look wider) than simply allocating blame.

All action is interaction

This is a point I was lucky enough to learn at an early stage in my career. All action is interaction means that we do not operate in a vacuum. What I do is influenced by the actions of others around me, and my actions in turn will influence, to a certain extent at least, the actions of others. We go about our business in a world where people influence each other, where people influence the circumstances in which they live and work and the circumstances influence the people. If we want to develop an adequate understanding of people and their problems, we need to bear in mind that we are dealing with complex interactive situations rather than individuals in isolation.

An important concept here is that of 'the person in context'. What this refers to is the need to recognize that, although each of us is a unique individual in our own right, we are all unique individuals in a social context. So, while I am a unique individual, I also am a member of a class group, a gender, an ethnic group and so on. There will be wider sociological factors that have a bearing on who I am and how I go about making my impression upon the world. It is not uncommon for people to forget about the person in context and focus all their attention on the individual, as if he or she lives outside of this context. Sometimes we can make the opposite mistake and see the context and put great emphasis on the significance of wider factors, but lose sight of the actual person at the heart of a situation. The key point to remember here is that we need to bear in mind the person *and* the context and not fall into the trap of looking at either the person or the context.

Another important dimension of this notion that all action is interaction is that problems will actually intertwine – that is, it would be naïve to look at particular problems in isolation. For example, the problem of one person being aggressive may be linked with another problem of someone else being subdued or even depressed. This is not necessarily to say that one problem causes the other, because sometimes they may cause each other or both may be caused by another set of circumstances. But, what it does mean is that we need to look at the big picture. We need to look at how problems may be interacting, perhaps reinforcing each other at times, cancelling each other out at others (although it has to be recognized that the former is much more common than the latter!). Someone who wants to be a skilled problem solver must therefore become accustomed to thinking more widely than seeing just individuals or just individual problems. One of the tools to be discussed in Part Two is that of helicopter vision, and this is a notion closely linked to the point I am making here – the need to get an overview or, as it is often called, 'the big picture'.

A third important point to note in relation to this central idea that all action is interaction is that the helper becomes part of the problem scenario – that is, in engaging with people who are experiencing problems, our input becomes part of the dynamic. This can be positive or negative, in the sense that our input can help, but can also hinder or even make the situation worse (see, for example, the discussion of the drama triangle in Part Two).

This third point is particularly important as it puts a lot of responsibility on our shoulders. When we enter a problem situation, it is to be hoped that we are doing so with the genuine intention of making the situation better or, where possible, resolving the problems we encounter. However, it also has to be recognized that our intervention can be detrimental. We can make a bad situation worse.

Problem identification

When we endeavour to tackle people problems, one thing we need to be very clear about is: what precisely is the problem we are tackling (or what are the problems)? A very common mistake is for people to try and come up with solutions before they have carefully worked out what the problem is. Sometimes the pressure of the problem situation leads us to feel that we need to come up with something very quickly. This can be quite dangerous, as we can often suggest or implement actions that are not appropriate. A key problem-solving skill, then, is the ability to resist the temptation to rush into attempting to provide solutions before we are clear what problem it is that we are dealing with.

Linked to this is the importance of establishing who it is a problem for. The significance of this lies in the fact that a situation could be problematic for different people in different ways. For example, in a situation involving conflict between two people, each of them may see the situation in very different terms and may have very different ideas about the nature, causes and possible solutions to the problem. A situation that can very commonly arise is where something can be a problem to one person, or group of people, but a benefit or a positive development for another person or another group. For example, where a project is cancelled, this may present significant headaches for one group of people but may be a source of great relief for another group who may have had doubts about their ability to fulfil the requirements of the project.

A further important point to consider in relation to problem identification is the need to take the problem to where the solution lies. What I mean by this is that there is little point focusing effort and attention on areas of a situation where a solution is not to be found. For example, if the solution to a particular problem relies on the provision of particular resources, then it will be necessary to take that problem to the person, or persons, who control those resources. To understand this further, consider the example of stress in the workplace. The traditional approach to stress is to perceive it as the sign of a weak individual, somebody who is not coping with the demands of their job. However, it is increasingly being recognized that stress is best seen in broader terms in relation to, for example, how the organization is managed. Giving a workload to somebody that he or she cannot cope with is not necessarily the sign of a weak individual, but could just as well be the sign of an organization that is being mismanaged (see the Health and Safety Executive Standards on workplace stress: www.hse.org.uk).

Motivation

Problem solving is something we do *with* people rather than *to* them. Therefore, it is important for them to have at least some degree of motivation to bring a resolution to the problems. To be an effective problem solver, we therefore need to have at least a basic understanding of motivation. It is beyond the scope of this book to provide a detailed exposition of what is involved in the complex psychology of motivation. However, what I can more realistically do is concentrate on four sets of issues and refer the interested reader to Part Three of the book where guidance on further learning in this area is provided.

1. *Pain versus pay-off* Very often the pain or suffering involved in a problem situation is enough to motivate the persons concerned to make the necessary changes. However, it is not

always that simple. Sometimes, despite the pain involved, the individual or individuals concerned may be receiving some sort of payoff or reward from the problem situation and this in itself can sustain it. For example, in a situation where somebody is developing a drink problem, he or she may be aware of the difficulties that this is causing and may wish to solve the problem, but the benefits that are derived from excessive drinking may stand in the way of this. Motivation, then, is not simply a matter of 'you've either got it or you haven't'. It can involve certain conflicts and, in particular, a trade-off between pain and pay-off.

2. *Balancing risks* People who are not motivated to tackle their problems often say that it is because they lack confidence in doing so. In my experience, lack of confidence can often derive from a person weighing up the risks of taking action and comparing this with what they perceive as the relatively easy option of doing nothing. However, this can be misleading. This is because there are risks involved in doing nothing. A more realistic approach, therefore, is to weigh up the risks involved in taking action compared with the risks involved in not taking action. Very often people become embroiled in a problem situation and can see the risks involved in trying to resolve it, but perhaps are less open to the suggestion that there are significant risks involved in not tackling their problems. A skilled problem solver can therefore often be involved in trying to help people get a more balanced perspective on the risks involved in their situation from the point of view of both taking action and not doing so.

3. *Resistance, change and grief* It is not uncommon for people to resist tackling their problems because to do so would involve some degree of change. When we enter into a change period in our life, particularly a significant amount of change, this can lead to a grief reaction. This is because even though the change may be very positive, we may lose certain things that we value as part of the change process. This is a point to which we shall return below in the section headed 'Promoting change'.

4. *Problem embedding* This is a term I use to refer to the process whereby trying to tackle one problem can bring us up against another problem, and trying to solve the second problem can bring us up against a third problem and so on. That is, sometimes problems are embedded within wider problems – in

the same way that Russian dolls are embedded one within the others. Where this 'problem embedding' occurs, it can be a real test of motivation. For example, someone can try very hard to solve the first problem, but when they realize that this leads to a second problem, they may give up. They may regard the situation as irresolvable rather than turn their problem-solving attention to the second problem they encounter. Practice focus 1.1 illustrates this.

Practice focus 1.1

Lin had a lot of experience of helping people solve their problems. She was aware that trying to solve one problem often unearthed another one. She was also aware that coming across a second problem would often lead to people giving up on the first – to adopt a defeatist attitude when they realized that one problem was embedded in another. She was therefore ready for this whenever the situation arose, as she could anticipate that it would be an issue. Her way of dealing with it was to make it clear from the beginning of her work with a particular individual or group that one problem might reveal another and that it would be important to then turn their attention to this second problem rather than give up. This did not guarantee that people would not become defeatist, but it did seem to lessen the chances of that happening, and it also gave her a good platform from which to challenge the defeatism if it did arise.

Problems not puzzles

Revans (1998) draws an important distinction between problems and puzzles. He argues that puzzles have a single, definitive solution. For example, in a crossword puzzle, there is only one correct answer (in principle) for each clue. A problem, by contrast, is something that can have many solutions. Each potential solution will have strengths and weaknesses, costs and benefits, advantages and disadvantages. It will rarely be the case that there is a solution that will be entirely positive without some sort of drawback. There are two key issues arising from this. First, there is the question of ownership. We have to remember whose problem it is. There is little point in our trying to impose our own solution on someone unless that person is committed to that particular solution. This is an example of working in partnership which will be discussed in more detail below in the section headed 'PRECISE practice'. What it involves is working with the individuals concerned but without taking over – without trying to impose our solution. It is more a case of working together to identify possible solutions, evaluating them and coming up with what is perceived as the best way forward.

Second, this means that different problem solvers will adopt different approaches. It certainly does not mean that it is inappropriate or unacceptable that you are adopting a different approach from that adopted by a colleague, for example. It does mean that all of us involved in people problems can learn from each other and benefit from each other's experiences, but we must avoid coming to the simplistic solution that there is one right answer or one correct approach. Each approach, as noted above, will have its strengths and weaknesses.

Promoting change

Problem solving can be seen as a process of moving from an undesirable situation to a more desirable one. Change is therefore essential to that process. When we are talking about problem solving, we are, of course, talking about promoting change. This can be seen to apply at six levels:

1. *Individuals* The resolution of very many problems involves changing the behaviour or attitudes of one or more individuals. Sometimes the behaviour of one person can cause problems for one or more others – for example, when a key person is behaving in an insensitive way. However, what can also occur is when an individual, through his or her behaviour and attitude, causes problems for him- or herself. An example of this would be somebody who perhaps adopts a confrontational attitude towards other people which results in a far higher level of conflict or even aggression than is necessary. The individual concerned may not realize that it is his or her behaviour that is leading to the problematic reaction being experienced.

2. *Families* The point was made earlier that individuals need to be understood in context. The family context is a big part of this. Even where an individual lives alone and not apparently as part of a family, it is unlikely that relationships with family

members or the influence of family members through upbringing, for example, will not still be a significant part of the situation. The family context is therefore an important part of understanding problems. This is largely because families develop a set of unwritten rules – their own culture, as it were. Families also tend to have sets of power relations and certain channels of communication. Problems can arise in relation to any of these – that is, culture, power relations and communication. What is also interesting, and important to note, is that problems within families can lead to problems elsewhere – for example, in the workplace. Someone who, within their own family, is in a relatively powerless position may therefore lack confidence in dealing with the exercise of power in the workplace. However, we should be careful not to oversimplify here, as the transfer of problems from one domain (that is, the family) to another (the workplace) is not inevitable.

3. *Groups* This can refer to formal groups, such as staff teams, project teams, committees and so on or, more importantly, to gatherings of people who come together for a particular purpose, or just by force of circumstance. A key concept here is that of group dynamics. There is an extensive literature (see Part Three) which addresses the way in which individuals, when combined in a group, can produce complex patterns of interaction. As with families, much of this can relate to cultures based on unwritten rules, power relations and communication.

4. *Communities* When an individual is experiencing problems, these can affect not just that individual and his or her immediate family and perhaps colleagues, but also the wider community. For example, somebody experiencing mental health problems can cause distress and concern within a community. However, it is not simply the case that individual problems can become translated into community problems; communities themselves can have problems – for example, as a result of the lack of certain resources or amenities. There may also be tensions or conflicts within a community, perhaps for historical reasons, perhaps linked to social problems like racism or sexism. It is sadly the case that the community level is often one that is neglected by many people in the people professions. It is a very easy mistake to make to concentrate predominantly on individuals, perhaps paying some attention to their family or work context, but without considering the

wider community, both in terms of how the individual can be affecting that community and how that community can be affecting the individual.

5. *Organizations* I have previously made the point (Thompson, 2003a) that organizations are dangerous places. What I mean by this is that organizations can have a very detrimental effect on us. For example, the organization we work for can have a hugely influential impact on our lives, sometimes in a negative way. Consider, for example, the following scenarios:

(a) An employee is devastated by being made redundant and is extremely worried about how he or she will be able to manage financially without a regular salary to rely on.

(b) A staff member is bullied by a manager to the extent that he or she becomes ill as a result of the stress involved.

(c) An applicant for promotion feels bitter, angry and distressed when his or her application is declined.

(d) A whole group of employees are extremely concerned when they are told that their team is to be disbanded as a result of reorganization.

Of course, these are not the only examples of how organizations can have a negative impact on people within them. Problems often have their roots in the way organizations work and the way they treat people. Although the idea of an organization is traditionally presented in very rational terms, in reality organizations are very emotive places. By this I mean that emotions play a very important role in how business is conducted and how organizational life is experienced by its participants. When the emotional dimension of organizations is neglected or mishandled, significant problems can arise.

6. *Society* Some problems can be seen to arise from the very workings of our society – that is, they have their roots in complex political and socioeconomic matters way beyond the scope of individuals. While as problem solvers we may be in no position (apart from voting every so often) to change the nature of society and its political workings, we can at least take account of them in understanding the complexities of the problems we deal with at the other five levels.

This brief overview of the six levels should be sufficient to paint a picture of just how complex the notion of promoting change is. One key point that I wish to emphasize is that it is important that we move away from the idea that promoting change is exclusively, or even predominantly, about promoting individual change. Very often the need for change lies elsewhere, and it would be foolish for us to ignore that fact.

PRECISE practice

PRECISE is an acronym for **p**artnership-based, **r**ealistic, **e**mpowering, **c**reative, **i**ntegrated, **s**ystematic and **e**ffective practice. This is a framework that I have devised to try and get across the point that good practice in problem solving needs to fit in with these seven areas. Let us look at each of them in turn.

Partnership based

The point was made earlier that there is little point in trying to impose a solution on people, as this is very unlikely to work. There are also ethical considerations about whether we have the right to try and impose a solution on somebody else. This approach is therefore best avoided. What is much more appropriate is an approach based on partnership. What this involves is working closely with the people concerned to:

(a) identify what the problem areas are;
(b) establish possible solutions;
(c) evaluate those solutions and choose the most appropriate way forward; and
(d) implement together, where appropriate, a plan of action.

In some circumstances, our role will be to help people understand how best to move forward and then leave them to implement the plan themselves. But in other circumstances, we will also have a role in working in partnership with them actually to implement the plan itself.

Realistic

This can be seen to apply in two senses. First of all, we need to be realistic in the sense of making sure that our proposed solutions are workable. It can be harmful and counterproductive to generate unrealistic expectations. We therefore have to make sure that our feet are firmly on the ground when it comes to tackling problems. We also need to be realistic in the sense referred to earlier – namely, to avoid the unhelpful extremes of pessimism and negativity on the one hand, and naïve optimism on the other. Realism, in my view, is the healthy balance between these two extremes. It involves recognizing that, in any situation, there will be positives, but there will also be negatives. The danger with pessimism is that we see the weaknesses, but fail to address the strengths. The problem with optimism is that we see the positives, but do not take adequate account of the negatives, thus leaving ourselves very vulnerable.

Empowering

Literally, the term 'empower' means to give power to. However, we cannot do this in a direct or literal sense. What empowerment is really about is helping people gain greater control over their lives and circumstances. This can involve helping them to recognize obstacles to progress, both within their own mind, where appropriate, and in their wider social circumstances – for example, if they are being discriminated against or disadvantaged in some way by other people. Empowerment also involves helping people solve their own problems rather than making them dependent on us. This is because, in the former case, the power mainly lies with the individual concerned. Once we leave the situation they are in control of their circumstances to a larger extent than they were before if our attempts at empowerment have worked. However, if we act in such a way that creates dependency, then this sets up a power relationship in which the person we are trying to help is actually less powerful because they are now in a subordinate relationship to ourselves. A key part of effective problem solving, then, is that we make sure that, as far as possible, we empower people to resolve their own difficulties rather than do it for them and, in the process, risk making them dependent on us.

An important part of this is to recognize people's strengths and seek to build on them. It is very easy, when dealing with problems, to lose sight of the strengths dimension and thereby adopt an unduly negative perspective on the situation being dealt with. We all have strengths to draw upon, but it is not unusual for the pressure of certain problem situations to cast a shadow over them, perhaps to the point where we forget to take them into consideration and make full use of them.

Similarly, resilience is a characteristic that can usefully be fostered as part of an ethos of empowerment. Being 'resilient' means being able to withstand pressures and adversity and, where possible, using the situation as a basis for developing new strengths – 'growing' as a result of the experience. The notion of resilience as part of empowerment helps us to appreciate that people problem solving is not about doing things to or for people, but rather doing what we can to help them resolve their own difficulties, to draw on their strengths and to use the experience to develop new strengths where possible.

Creative

In the very pressurized work settings in which so many people professionals operate, it is very easy to get into habits and patterns, to get into a rut. This can be very destructive in a number of ways – for example, in the detrimental effect it can have on morale. Another problem that it causes is that such an approach closes off our ability to be creative, to find a range of potential solutions and to explore these together, rather than simply to opt for the first solution that comes to mind.

There is a common stereotype that associates creativity with being artistic. This is misleading as some of the world's greatest scientists have been very creative indeed. Art may indeed involve creativity, but creativity does not need to involve art. Being creative means not getting stuck in ruts and coming up with standard solutions. It involves being able to look carefully at a situation and to be able to generate a number of different outlooks, a number of different ways forward.

Integrated

In many situations, there will be more than one person trying to help. If we are not careful, this can lead to a very fragmented approach, where some people's efforts actually get in the way of or counteract the efforts of others. It is therefore important that we adopt an integrated approach – that is, one which takes account of the various issues involved, the various people involved, rather than working in an isolated, fragmented way. This is more easily said than done, but the efforts required to adopt an integrated approach are none the less, well worth the investment of time and energy involved.

Systematic

Systematic practice is a concept discussed in *People Skills* (Thompson, 2002a). In a nutshell, it refers to the importance of being clear at all times about what we are trying to achieve, how we intend to achieve it and how we will know when we have achieved it. This is very important because, without such a framework, it is very easy for the pressures and demands of the job to push us into a situation where we lose focus, we drift and become prey to a great many distractions. If you are not familiar with the concept of systematic practice, it is highly recommended that you read the relevant chapters in *People Skills*.

Effective

It perhaps goes without saying that there is no point in putting a great deal of time, effort and energy into attempting to resolve problems unless we are to be effective in doing so. The reality of the situation is that some problems, despite our best efforts, cannot be resolved. However, it is vitally important that we 'give it our best shot' and try to make sure that our efforts are as effective as possible. Much of this will come from the accumulation of experience and wisdom. However, there is also much to be gained, even for those of us in the early stages of our people problem-solving careers, to maintain a clear focus on the principles underlying our practice, and make sure that, in being 'precise', we are maximizing the chances of being effective.

Problems and challenges

Tackling problems involves coming face to face with certain challenges. Indeed, it could be argued that one of the rewards of being a people problem solver is that there can be great pleasure and satisfaction derived from rising to, and meeting, challenges. In order to understand the complexities of problems and challenges, it can be helpful to divide challenges into three categories: existential, interpersonal and sociopolitical.

Existential challenges

This refers to the type of challenges that we face simply by being human beings, by being in the world and seeking to make sense of it – our 'spiritual journey', as it were, of finding our way through life and maintaining a thread of meaning through it (Moss, 2005). These involve the challenges of growing up, developing our own identity, finding our place in the world, coping with the anguish or 'angst' involved in transitions and losses, and so on. While these may be experienced differently by different people, they are the sort of challenges that, by and large, we all face as we work our way through life. The emphasis here, then, is on rising to these challenges rather than avoiding them. Existential challenges can generally be seen as crises or turning points in our life – for example, adolescence. Making the transition from childhood to adulthood may well present us with certain problems, but there are also tremendous gains to be made. Responding to existential challenges therefore will often involve trying to make the best of the situation to maximize the positive potential of the crisis (Thompson, 1991). These are the sort of challenges that we all have to go through at some time or another, and so there is a wealth of wisdom and experience to be drawn on in dealing with these.

However, balanced against that, it must be remembered that each of us will experience a crisis in our own personal way. However much we may have in common with others who have experienced similar crises, it still remains our own personal crisis, a unique experience for each of us.

Interpersonal challenges

Based on the theme of 'all action is interaction', as discussed above, we can recognize that many of the challenges we face in life are interpersonal challenges. By this I mean that they arise from our relationships with other people. We live in a social world and this means that other people play an important role in our lives, whether we like it or not. Many problems arise as a result of conflict, and this in turn is frequently due to interpersonal issues.

In many cases, helping people to solve their problems involves a large amount of work geared towards managing relationships.

Sociopolitical challenges

These are the types of challenge that arise because of who we are in relation to broader society. They are connected to such matters as 'social location'. This refers to our position in the social hierarchy in terms of power relations connected with, for example, race, class and gender. An example of a sociopolitical challenge would be that of dealing with poverty. We all have the challenge of making ends meet but, for some people, their social circumstances mean that this is a much greater struggle than it is for the majority of other people. Traditional approaches to people and their problems have tended to individualize matters, to focus on what relates to specific unique individuals. And, while recognizing the uniqueness of the individual is clearly important, this also has to be balanced out by recognition that each person is an individual in a social context. We can produce a very distorted perspective on the situation if we ignore the social context, as argued earlier. However, I am not simply reiterating that point here, I am making the related point that often the challenges we encounter are not only experienced in a social context but *arise from* that context.

Practice focus 1.2

Rachid undertook a project on depression as part of his course. He obtained permission to interview a number of people who attended a mental health day centre and who had been diagnosed as suffering from depression. He felt it would be better in terms of privacy and confidentiality to carry out the interviews in people's own homes rather than at the centre. This proved to be a very significant decision as it meant that Rachid visited the homes of several members of the day centre – and from this he saw for himself the powerful role social circumstances can play in people's problems. He saw evidence of considerable poverty and deprivation, very poor-quality housing, stigma and discrimination, high crime rates and little social cohesion. He began to think that he would be depressed if he lived in circumstances like that. When he discussed the situation with his tutor, the point was emphasized that, in order to understand a person's problems, we need to understand issues relating to the individual *and* to his or her social circumstances, and that we should be careful not to oversimplify by looking at one set of issues without considering the other.

To connect this with another point made earlier, this is another reason why it is important not to adopt a judgemental attitude, as often what are perceived as personal inadequacies on the part of a particular individual may owe more to the social circumstances of that individual than to any personal characteristics.

The problem-solving process

Perhaps a more appropriate title for this section would be *a* problem-solving process. This is because there is no single, definitive approach. As I argued earlier, we are dealing with problems, not puzzles, and so there will be a multiplicity of ways in which we can tackle the issues arising and there is no simple right or wrong to this. We are dealing with much more complex issues than that. It is important to emphasize, then, that what I am presenting here is not a dogmatic approach, but rather a set of guidelines based on experience and research which I have found to be useful in my own extensive experience of problem solving and in my equally extensive experience of teaching others how to tackle such problems.

The process can be divided into a number of sections or subsections. I shall discuss each of them in turn.

Information gathering

It is dangerous to try and tackle problems in the dark. We need to have information about key aspects of the situation. We need to gather information about people's perception of the problem(s), their feelings about them and reactions to them, the factors that appear to be significant, and so on. Knowing what information to gather is a skill that takes time to develop. To explore these issues further, a useful starting point would be the chapter on 'Assessment' in *People Skills*.

Analysis and problem definition

Gathering information can lead us to a situation where we have a lot of data, but it does not really tell us anything. This is where the analysis comes in. It involves piecing together the relevant bits of information, forming patterns, making sense of what we see. From this, we can then start to engage in the process of problem definition:

What precisely is the problem/are the problems? Who is it a problem for? and so on, as discussed earlier. An important pitfall to avoid here is that of drowning in information. This seems to be a characteristic of our modern age – the fact that we have access to so much information. On occasions, problem solvers can cause problems for themselves by gathering so much information that they do not know what to do with it. They fall into the trap of gathering as much information as possible rather than gathering the relevant information they need. Well-developed analytical skills can therefore be seen as an important part of the effective problem solver's repertoire.

Identification of strengths and opportunities

It is very easy when dealing with problems to focus predominantly, or even exclusively, on the negatives, to fail to see that situations also involve strengths and opportunities. This is something that will be discussed in more detail in Part Two under the heading of 'SWOT analysis'. However, at this point, it is important to emphasize that we should not allow ourselves to produce an unbalanced assessment of the situation that fails to take account of the positives as well as the negatives.

Exploration of possible solutions

Following on from our discussion earlier of the importance of creativity in problem solving, we can note that there is much to be gained from exploring a range of possible solutions, rather than simply opting for the first one that comes to mind. The chances of the first solution that occurs to us being the best one possible are clearly pretty slim. We therefore have to be careful that we do not allow our anxieties to produce a fairly rapid solution to a problem or set of problems to lead us into a situation where we fail to consider other options.

Evaluation of possible solutions

Once we have a good understanding of the potential solutions, the next step is to weigh them up, to work out which in the circumstances is likely to be the best way forward (or which combination of solutions is likely to be the most effective). It should be remembered that this evaluation needs to be undertaken in partnership – that is, we need to work together with the people concerned to identify what is likely to work best. It is not simply a matter of our prescribing the cure.

Formulate a plan

Sometimes gathering information about a problem, analysing it, and discussing this with the person concerned, can be enough to free them up to take the initiative and resolve matters. However, this is not always the case and, in many circumstances, what is needed is to formulate a plan of action. Having evaluated the possible solutions, we now need to look at such matters as the timescales involved, who is going to be responsible for what, and so on (this links closely with systematic practice as discussed above). Having a plan is very important because, on the one hand, it helps to maintain a structure and discipline to the work being undertaken – it prevents drift and a lack of focus. On the other hand, it also enables us to monitor progress and to ensure that we are in fact heading in the right direction.

There is no need for the plan to be rigidly adhered to if it is not working, as there is always scope to review the plan. However, at this stage, it is important to map out the route we intend to follow to arrive at the problem resolution. It is unlikely that we will simply arrive there without having first worked out our route plan.

Revisit the information and analysis

Before implementing the plan that we have formulated, we just need to make one further quick check. We need to go back to the information that we gathered and the analysis of it that we performed, partly to reassure ourselves that we have got it right before we start taking important steps forward, and partly to see whether the situation has changed or is changing, as we go through the problem-solving process.

Implement the plan

Once we have reassured ourselves that we have produced the right information and analysis as far as we possibly can in the circumstances, we are now ready to implement the plan, to take the steps identified in that plan in order to work towards our desired outcomes.

Monitor and review

People and circumstances change, and so it is essential that we keep the situation under review. It would be very naïve indeed, and it would also be dangerous, simply to allow situations to move on without keeping a clear focus on whether things are moving in the desired direction. Often, what enables us to be effective problem solvers is that our presence and support can give a sense of confidence and security to the people experiencing the problems. If we fail to monitor and review the situation, then that confidence can be lost. That security can disappear and we can very quickly find ourselves back at square one, having wasted a lot of time, effort and energy. In so doing, we may also have 'blown it' in terms of any future work because, if in failing to monitor and review, we have lost the trust of the people concerned, then it is going to be very difficult, if not impossible, to regain that trust.

Conclude involvement when appropriate

A very clear trend that I have noticed in works which discuss problem solving or helping processes is that they often fail to mention the conclusion or termination of that process. It is as if it is assumed that work will continue indefinitely. Given our discussions above of empowerment and the need to avoid creating dependency, clearly this is highly problematic. Considerable attention therefore needs to be given to the question of when and how to draw involvement to a close. Timing will be important. We do not wish to withdraw too soon and run the risk of our good work unfurling. Nor do we wish to stay involved longer than is necessary, thus wasting our own time resources and risking creating dependency. How to conclude is also important. There are skills involved in how to bring our involvement to an end.

Problems and opportunities

You will probably be familiar with the idea that 'there's no such thing as a problem, only an opportunity'. This idea is both inaccurate and dangerous. If we were to say that problems also present opportunities, then that is something that I would fully agree with. However, to argue that there is no such thing as a problem, only an opportunity, is naïve in the extreme.

Reference was made earlier to the notion of crisis, a turning point in somebody's life – a situation that cannot stay the same. It will either get better or get worse. Often the problems that people encounter are indeed crises and, as such, they can be quite threatening, but they can also be a gateway to growth, improvement and development. A skilled and experienced people problem solver will therefore be trying to capitalize on problem situations, particularly those that are crises, in order to maximize the positive potential to bring out the silver linings, as it were. This is something that has to be handled carefully and sensitively. For example, when somebody is very distressed or worried about their situation, if we are trying to be positive about the situation in an insensitive, ill-thought through way, we may only serve to alienate that person from us. They may see us as somebody who does not understand what they are going through because we are trying to put a positive gloss on something that they perhaps find acutely painful. We should therefore be wary of tackling these issues in an insensitive way. They call for very careful and sensitive handling.

Reflective practice

The final chapter of *People Skills* is devoted to the topic of reflective practice. This is an approach to professional practice and management which seeks to avoid the extremes of (i) adopting a mechanistic approach to the use of professional knowledge (research, for example) and (ii) of rejecting the professional knowledge base in favour of a 'common sense' approach. There are two ill-informed and ill-advised schools of thought. There is the school of thought that sees research, theory and professional knowledge more broadly as the source of 'the answers', and adherents of this school are often disappointed because the knowledge base does not tell them precisely what they need to know. It does not give them a clear plan of action to follow. At the other extreme is a school of thought that says 'I prefer to stick to practice', as if research, theory and professional knowledge have got nothing to do with the work they undertake. In between these two dangerous extremes is reflective practice. Reflective practice involves a number of things but for present purposes, I shall concentrate on three in particular; three that are very relevant to this particular book.

1. *Not just using tools mechanistically* The point was made earlier that the tools provided in Part Two of the book will not do the job for us. They are a means to an end, but they cannot be relied upon to do our work for us. One of the tenets of reflective practice is that we need to act like skilled tailors cutting the cloth of the professional knowledge base to suit the specific measurements and requirements of the garment we are trying to create. That is, we need to draw on the professional knowledge base in such a way that it fits the specific practice realities – the problems we are seeking to solve – as closely as possible.

2. *Art and craft* Traditional approaches to research and theory have tended to emphasize science and rationality, but the proponents of reflective practice (for example, Schön, 1983) have emphasized the art and craft involved. What this refers to is that the knowledge and understanding available to us have to be crafted to suit circumstances, just as an artist or a craftsperson has to draw on a set of skills and the benefit of experience in order to produce the desired outcome. But, to return to the point I made earlier, it is important not to confuse the creativity involved with being an actual artist. In parallel fashion, having a degree in science and technology does not make someone into an engineer. It may provide them with much of the core knowledge that they need to be an engineer, but actually achieving the status of an engineer means developing the artistry and the craft skills to be able to use that knowledge in practice. This is very much what reflective practice is about, not simply having the knowledge but having the craft skills to be able to use it appropriately in real life problem-solving situations, whether we are engineers working with materials and natural substances, or problem solvers in people professions working with people.

3. *Analytical skills* The point was made earlier that well-developed analytical skills are an important part of a problem solver's repertoire. This is largely because analysis is a key part of reflective practice. To be a reflective practitioner, we need to be able to make sense of the complex realities we deal

with, to be able to cut through the confusion and the indeterminacy, as Schön calls it, of real life situations. We need to be able to create a picture of what we are dealing with that is sufficiently clear to enable us and the people we are working with to understand the nature of the problems and the possible solutions.

Reflective practice, then, is clearly an important basis for good practice in working with people and their problems.

It is important to recognize that some problems are more difficult than others to solve and that some may not be capable of resolution at all. An important concept to note in this regard is what Clarke and Stewart (2003) describe as 'wicked issues':

> Wicked problems . . . are those for which there is no obvious or easily found solution. They seem intractable. . . . There can be hope that wicked problems will be solved over time, but that requires learning of the nature of the problems and of their causes. They require a capacity to derive and design new approaches for their resolution and to learn of their impact. They are likely to be resolved not directly but through an iterative process – learning, trying and learning. (p. 274)

They go on to comment on how such problems can be addressed:

> Tackling wicked issues therefore requires:
>
> - holistic not partial or linear thinking, capable of encompassing the interaction of a wide variety of activities, habits, behaviour and attitudes;
> - a capacity to think outside and work across organizational boundaries;
> - ways of involving the public in developing responses;
> - embracing a willingness to think and work in completely new ways. While most people will come to this trapped or constrained by conventional organizations, labels and assumptions, what is needed is willingness to entertain the unconventional and pursue the radical. (p. 275)

The idea of an iterative process plus the notion of being willing to think and work in new ways are both strongly consistent with reflective practice. A reflective approach to the complex, often ingrained problems we so often encounter can be therefore be seen as a much better option than a mechanistic approach that seeks to apply a similar formula or that tries to achieve a simple solution. The fact that so many of the 'people problems' we deal with can be seen as 'wicked', in Clarke and Stewart's sense, shows how important it is to adopt an approach premised on reflective practice.

Operacy

Operacy is a term introduced by Edward de Bono (de Bono, 1983), the writer best known for his work on lateral thinking (de Bono, 1990). He presents it as a term parallel with literacy and numeracy. Literacy refers to the ability to use words to good effect. Numeracy, similarly, refers to the ability to use numbers appropriately. Operacy refers to our actions and is used by de Bono to mean the ability to get things done, to 'make things happen'. While we can never guarantee success in our problem-solving endeavours, we can at least adopt a 'can do' attitude, a positive commitment to achieving the outcomes we seek as far as we reasonably can.

Operacy and a 'can do' attitude are the opposite of the defeatism, cynicism and 'learned helplessness' that is unfortunately far too common in some sectors of the helping professions. We are often trying to make progress in very difficult circumstances, perhaps having to struggle by without the resources we need and not receiving the support, appreciation or recognition we deserve, and so it is understandable that there is a tendency to feel cynical and defeatist. However, the fact that it is understandable does not make it acceptable. This is because a negative, defeatist attitude makes it less likely that we will be able to help people solve their problems rather than more. And, as noted above, given that our intervention can actually make people's problems worse in some circumstances, adopting a defeatist attitude is a very dangerous undertaking.

If we are being defeatist or cynical because we are feeling stressed, then I would argue strongly that we are duty bound to take steps to deal with that stress, rather than allow the people we are trying to help lose out because of our own problems.

Practice focus 1.3

Robbie had been in post for just over a year when his enthusiasm started to wane. Within a few months he was at a very low ebb indeed – he had become quite cynical and defeatist. His supervisor should have been in a position to help him tackle the issues, but he too was at a low ebb and they were both part of a culture of cynicism and defeatism that had developed over time. Things came to a head for Robbie when he applied for a post in another department within his office and was not even shortlisted for it. When he sought feedback from the section head in the department he had applied to work in about why he had not been shortlisted, he was told quite clearly and firmly that there was no room in that department for people who were paid to help others with problems, but who appeared to make no attempt to solve their own difficulties.

Conclusion

Part One has covered a wide range of issues, and it could be argued that it has not done justice to any of them. However, my intention here has not been to provide an in-depth exposition of problem solving. That would be far too unrealistic in the space available. Rather, my intention has been to provide an overview which will, it is to be hoped, alert you to some of the complexities involved and give you a framework for developing your studies of problem solving in greater depth and breadth. In this respect, this book parallels *People Skills* which provides an introductory overview to a wide range of skills, but does not have the luxury of examining any of them in any great detail. That is a task that must be left to other texts and other occasions.

My advice to you would be to begin now to explore the methods, techniques and tools in Part Two. Once you begin to read each of them, if it is something that appeals to you, then please read it in detail and take careful note of what it is about. If it is something that, for some reason, does not appeal to you, then feel free to move on to the next one. It is unlikely that all readers will find all fifty tools to their liking or suitable for their style of working. That is not a problem. Of the fifty presented, there is likely to be plenty of value for everyone. I would also suggest that, once you have finished working your way through Part Two, you return to Part One and re-read it. Reading something for a second time will in itself give you a greater depth of understanding but, reading it after having read Part Two, is likely to give you an even deeper understanding, as I anticipate that many of the points I have made in Part One will come to life much more fully once you have read (and better still, implemented) the tools and strategies presented. Once you have re-read Part One, you should then be in a strong position to engage with Part Three and to follow up on those references, websites and so on that will offer you further food for thought, debate, analysis and learning. Indeed, there is a huge theory base underpinning the ideas presented in this book. It would not be realistic to attempt to cover that vast and complex theory base within the book itself, but it would certainly be wise for you to follow up at least some of the suggestions for further reading, as there is so much more that can be learned about this demanding but rewarding field of practice in dealing with people and their problems.

PART TWO

Problem-Solving
Methods

Introduction

Part Two of the book contains fifty 'tools' – methods or techniques that can be used to help tackle problems. They are geared towards 'operacy', as discussed in Part One, Edward de Bono's notion of 'making things happen'. Achieving our goals often depends on being able to solve problems – for example, removing barriers to progress. Problem solving, then, is not a peripheral activity – much of what happens in various work settings is about problem solving. So many of these problems are 'people' problems, in the sense that they relate to human factors, such as relationships, emotions and needs. Many of the problems that appear on the surface to be technical problems may also have their roots in the 'people' dimension.

No tool is guaranteed to work, but when used skilfully and in the appropriate circumstances, these techniques should significantly increase the chances of success. How you use the tools will be a key factor. To assist you with this, for each of the techniques you should consider the following before putting the ideas into practice:

1. *What are the key ideas?* Are you sure you understand them? It would be dangerous to proceed to using the tool without a proper grasp of the ideas involved.
2. *In what circumstances does it apply?* What would make you select this particular item from your toolkit? It is important to match the technique to the circumstances, rather than just rely on trial and error.
3. *In what circumstances would it not apply?* Of course, not all tools will apply in all circumstances. Are there any

'contra-indications' about a particular tool for the issues you are trying to deal with?

4. *What preparation is needed?* Is there anything you need to do or put in place before using this particular method? A good tool used at a bad time could be very problematic. Doing the necessary preparation could make all the difference in some cases.

5. *What support is needed?* Do you have the necessary back up? If you are not very experienced, do you have a more experienced colleague or manager to consult or gain support from? Do not leave yourself vulnerable and unsupported unnecessarily.

6. *What do I need to be wary about?* Are there any pitfalls to avoid? Forewarned is, of course, forearmed. Avoid getting yourself into difficulties that could have been anticipated (and thus avoided) if you had thought ahead. In using these tools, it is also worth remembering that your role is one of facilitator, in the sense that it is not up to you to solve the problems yourself, but rather to help the people concerned to do so. 'Problem management facilitation' may be a bit of a mouthful, but the reality is that this is what tackling people problems is all about.

It is also worth remembering the role of power and the dangers of discrimination. Whether you are using the tools presented here or any other for that matter, you will need to bear in mind that, whenever we are dealing with people, there is the possibility for discrimination and disadvantage to creep in (see Thompson, 2003a and 2006 for a discussion of these issues). Make sure that, at all times, you are:

- not relying on stereotypes or making assumptions about people;
- not being judgemental;
- looking at the situation from their point of view and not imposing your own;
- taking account of the role of discrimination in people's lives and recognizing that it can be a key factor in the problems people are experiencing;
- valuing difference and diversity – rather than distancing yourself from people because they are in some way different from you; and
- promoting equality by ensuring that everyone is dealt with fairly.

It is likely that, the less experienced you are, the more you will get out of this book, but it is to be hoped that even very experienced practitioners and managers will gain something from it. I anticipate that more experienced readers will gain most benefit when they are feeling 'stuck' with a particular problem. That is, when there is a problem that is exercising their thoughts a great deal, but little or no progress is being made, revisiting the tools here may give fresh insights and offer a way forward.

A note on working with children and adolescents

Many of these tools can be used in working with children and adolescents – indeed, some of them can be particularly effective when used with children ('Consequences', for example). However, if you work with children and young people, it will be important for you to consider the stage of development of the individual(s) concerned and make a professional judgement about which of these tools are appropriate and in what circumstances. If you are in any doubt, seek the advice of a senior colleague.

Avoiding avoidance
Facing up to our responsibilities

'Avoidance behaviour' is an important concept in the world of tackling people problems. This is because the sorts of problems that people encounter often generate a degree of anxiety, and that anxiety can lead people to try to avoid circumstances they face rather than to tackle them. Avoidance behaviour can take two main forms. First of all, there is direct avoidance behaviour. This is where we know something is problematic for us and we deliberately steer clear of it. In some circumstances that can be a very healthy and helpful way of dealing with the issues. However, in a wide range of other circumstances, this can be problematic because it means that we do not actually engage in problem-solving behaviours, and so the problem persists, perhaps getting worse over time.

The second type of avoidance behaviour is denial. This is where we try to deceive ourselves into thinking that there is no problem.

This is sometimes referred to as the ostrich approach – putting our head in the sand and hoping that, if we cannot see the problem, then it cannot exist. Naïve though this approach may be, it is none the less very common. What tends to happen in such circumstances is that the problem situation creates anxiety and we deal with that anxiety by putting some distance between ourselves and whatever it is that is raising the anxiety in the first place. One very sad thing to note about denial is that, ironically, it can lead to situations where people who could have helped us will not help us, because they are, in effect, taken in by our denial. If we deny that there is a problem and somebody who could have helped us to resolve the problem accepts our denial, then we have missed the opportunity of perhaps gaining some very valuable help.

As we shall see later in the discussion of 'Know your enemy', it is helpful to translate generalized anxiety into specific fears, and this can certainly be a good way of 'avoiding avoidance'. However, there are other means of doing so.

One potentially very effective way of tackling avoidance behaviour is through sharing. As anxiety is a significant factor in the root cause of avoidance behaviour, then anxiety can best be tackled jointly. This could apply in terms of your joining with the anxious person in a shared endeavour to deal with the issues affecting them. This may give them the confidence to go beyond avoidance. However, this can also be done through developing mutual support systems. For example, you could consider bringing together a number of people who share the same problem so that they feel more confident in tackling issues together. This is the basis of support groups (see 'Brokerage').

Some of the other tools in this book can also be useful in tackling avoidance behaviour. For example, risk assessment and the consequences technique can help to establish the potential costs of not tackling problems by playing avoidance games.

This is not an exhaustive list, but it should be sufficient to help you think about the range of ways in which avoidance behaviour can be addressed.

In trying to deal with avoidance behaviour, it is important that we consider it at three levels. First of all, we need to ask 'Am I doing it?' Being a problem solver does not make you immune to this difficulty. There may be aspects of the work you do that you feel uncomfortable with and that you will avoid if possible. If that is the case, then you need to ask yourself 'Is this helping me or is it hindering me?'; 'Is my development being hampered by the fact that I feel uncomfortable about facing up to certain issues?' You may then need to consider adopting a problem-solving approach yourself to look at what steps you need to take to get over this type of unhelpful avoidance behaviour.

We also need to ask the question 'Is the person I'm trying to help doing it?' If the answer is yes, then we need to look carefully at what steps we can take to help them avoid falling into this trap. We should handle this very carefully, as avoidance may be acting as a form of crutch and, while it is not healthy to rely on crutches in the long run, taking away somebody's crutch before they feel confident to walk unaided could prove disastrous. They may need to be weaned off it, rather than have it taken away in what could come across as a fairly brutal attack – even if this is certainly not what you intended.

The third question we need to ask is 'Is the group of people doing it?' As we shall discuss in more detail below, there is an important psychological concept known as 'groupthink' (Janis, 1982). This refers to the tendency of groups of people to develop like-minded thinking to the extent that it becomes strongly established as part of their culture, even though such thinking may at times be unhelpful. For example, one member of a group may be thinking that the course of action that has been agreed is not a good one, but is reluctant to say so because being part of the group is more important than making the right choice of action. In this respect the group bonding, as it were, becomes problematic. People become reluctant to challenge any aspect of the group's thinking or actions for fear of disrupting the group – for fear of being seen as a potential outsider to the group. Groupthink commonly manifests itself as avoidance behaviour. That is, a whole group of people may be avoiding something important and, while certain individuals within the group may recognize the danger of this, they do not raise it because of the power of groupthink.

An important consideration when looking at avoiding avoidance is whether what is being avoided is something that can actually be dealt with. This is an important consideration because, in some circumstances, it is quite appropriate to avoid certain things, because there is nothing we can do about them and if we engage with them, they are likely to do us harm. For example, if we know that going to a certain part of a certain town late at night is likely to lead to violence, then avoiding being there is actually quite wise and is certainly not a problem to be solved. The key question to ask, therefore, is: 'Is that which is being avoided something that can be dealt with?' In other words, are people missing out on potential progress by not being prepared to face up to the problems that they are experiencing?

I have chosen to begin Part Two of the book with this particular tool because I see it as one that, if we are not careful, can undermine everything that follows. That is, the other forty-nine tools presented here will be of little value if avoidance behaviour means that people are not prepared to address the problems they face. If we want to make a success of people problem solving, then we have to become very competent at 'avoiding avoidance'. We need to be very wary of this significant danger of trying to distance ourselves from the issues that are causing harm. We need, over time, to develop fairly in-depth knowledge and a set of skills to help us ensure that avoidance is not part of our own work; is not something that is preventing progress for individuals whom we are trying to help, and is not a characteristic of groups or teams that can cause them major difficulties.

Brokerage
Redirecting people to sources of help

A longstanding tradition in the human services is the idea that the greatest tool that any professional worker has available to them is their own self. Hence the notion discussed below of use of self as a tool in its own right (see 'Modelling and use of self'). However, what is important for us to realize is that, beyond ourselves as a resource, we could have access to a vast range of other resources, in principle at least. Just as an insurance broker does not provide insurance services him- or herself, a 'people problems broker' can look for access to a wide range of other services or resources that may be very helpful in dealing with the problems being addressed.

In order to be able to use brokerage to good effect, we have to be able to move away from the assumption that we are responsible for solving other people's problems. We are, as mentioned in the introduction to Part Two of this book, 'problem-solving management facilitators'. This means that we share with others the responsibility for solving problems and, at the end of the day, the ultimate responsibility for a problem lies with the person who is experiencing it. We all have our own lives to lead. We must therefore not become precious about the problems we are trying to help people to solve. In many situations, there may well be others who are far better placed to deal with the issues than we are. Our challenge, then, is twofold: first, to be able to recognize those situations where someone else may be better suited to helping; second, to be able to make the necessary referral (with the consent of the individual concerned, of course) or to redirect the individual concerned.

Naturally, in order to be able to do this, we have to have a knowledge of what other resources and possibilities are available. This does not mean that we are expected to have an encyclopaedic knowledge of the possibilities available, but we should at least know the basics and, just as importantly, know how to find out more. Do you know what sources of help are available in your area? Do you know who offers what and do you know how to find out – how to fill the gaps in your knowledge?

Help with problems can come from a variety of sources. Consider, for example, the following:

- *Within the workplace* Sources of help here would include perhaps employee assistance programmes, occupational health and trade union support.
- *The statutory sector* Government bodies such as social services and the health service can provide a range of services that could be very helpful in certain circumstances.
- *The voluntary sector* There is a huge network of voluntary organizations ranging quite considerably in size and scope. All, however, have as their basic raison d'être a commitment to addressing particular problems.
- *The private sector* There are various organizations that offer problem-solving help in one form or another, for a fee.
- *Informal sources of support* This would include help from family, friends, colleagues, and so on.

A very common obstacle to people using the help that is available to them is the notion of stigma. Often this is misguided. For example, there is a common assumption that someone who receives counselling is in some way mentally disturbed or inadequate. Similarly, some people feel that if they accept help from a voluntary body (Relate, for example), then this somehow makes them a 'charity case'. Part of a brokerage role may therefore be clearing up any misconceptions or stereotypes about the nature of the help that can be offered and what accepting such help would actually mean.

Another important part of brokerage is making sure that, in referring or redirecting someone to another source of help, appropriate information is communicated. For example, I have come across a number of cases where someone has made a referral to a particular helping agency, but has not made it clear how significant or pressing the problem is, only for the agency receiving the referral to put it at the bottom of their priority list, often with disastrous consequences. We cannot blame another agency for not acting appropriately or sufficiently swiftly when we have not given them sufficient information to make it clear what is required in the circumstances.

In the spirit of partnership, as discussed in Part One, it is important that the person you are trying to help is fully aware of what you are proposing and is fully in agreement with it. Initial reluctance or resistance may need to be overcome through further discussion and clarification but, at the end of the day, it is pointless trying to make a referral to another source of help without the commitment of the person concerned, as clearly any such efforts will be doomed to failure if the individual concerned is not committed to making it work.

Another danger to be aware of in undertaking a brokerage role is the pitfall of what could be described as fobbing people off. If you do not take your brokerage role seriously, it can be perceived by the person who has asked for your help as a case of your fobbing them off, simply redirecting them to another source of help because you cannot be bothered to deal with the situation yourself. As you can imagine, this can lead to a great deal of ill-feeling and can cause a number of problems. It is therefore important, when you feel it is appropriate to refer somebody on to another source of support, that you make it perfectly clear what you are doing and why you are doing it, and do not leave that person with the impression that you are deflecting them onto somebody else.

Capitalizing on crisis
Realizing the potential of critical moments in a person's life

Crisis intervention is a longstanding, well-established approach in the caring professions in general, and mental health services in particular. It is based on what is known as crisis theory. The key elements of crisis theory are as follows:

1. A crisis is a turning point in somebody's life. It refers to a situation that may get better or may get worse, but it will not stay the same.
2. At a time of a crisis, the people involved are more likely to take steps that can have a significant impact on their situation. That is, somebody who is not in a crisis may be resistant to change but, when a crisis arises, he or she is likely to be more willing to take steps to alleviate or resolve the situation.
3. Because of (2) above, individuals in crisis can be very vulnerable to external influences and may need protecting from harmful influences — for example, people who may be seeking to exploit them in some way.
4. A crisis can generate a considerable amount of emotional energy. This energy can be positive and constructive or negative and destructive, depending on how it is managed by the individual concerned and the influence of others involved.
5. Where an individual is in crisis, he or she is likely to need help sooner rather than later. This is because the crisis situation is likely to be short term (crises by their very nature are short-term events) and opportunities could be missed to make changes to factors within the problem situation that perhaps gave rise to the crisis (based on Thompson, 1991).

The idea of capitalizing on crisis is based on the fact that people are more willing to make changes to their life and circumstances during the crisis than they might otherwise be. For example, somebody who is not very assertive, and who has experienced significant difficulties in their life because of this lack of assertion, may become more assertive in a crisis as if the emotional energy generated propels them forward. Similarly, somebody who is normally resistant to taking advice from others, perhaps in the arrogant view that no one has anything they can teach them, is likely to be more willing to listen to what others have to say when experiencing a crisis.

A very important issue here is keeping a clear focus on our role as a problem solver. We have to remember that our task is to help the individual, or individuals, concerned to deal with their problems. If we lose this focus, we can very easily exploit the individuals concerned by trying to use the crisis to manoeuvre them into a position that is more convenient or beneficial for us. We have to be very careful that we do not fall into the trap of kicking somebody while they are down. Helping somebody in crisis is a matter of trust. If that individual is prepared to accept help, then we have to be very careful to ensure that we do not abuse the trust involved. It takes a lot of courage for somebody to ask for help, and we should be careful to ensure that we do not exploit that courage inappropriately.

The basic idea behind crisis intervention is that we do, indeed, capitalize on the crisis; that we use the energy generated to move in a positive direction to resolve difficulties, make progress and, it is to be hoped, achieve an outcome that is an improvement on the original situation. Practice focus 2.1 illustrates this.

Timing is very important in capitalizing on crisis. By its very nature, a crisis is a temporary event. If an individual is going through a crisis, then it is likely that some sort of resolution will be achieved in a relatively short period of time. However, if we are not careful, that resolution will be a negative outcome rather than a positive one. This is because the tension involved in being in crisis can often lead people to taking inappropriate, unhelpful or counterproductive steps in order to get themselves out of it. This may have the effect of making the situation worse or, at least, perpetuating the problem. A crisis, in itself, will therefore not guarantee a positive outcome. The task of the problem solver is to analyse the situation carefully and look at how the positive energy generated can be used to make progress. If we are too slow to respond to the crisis, we may find that we have, in effect, missed the boat – that the person concerned has already taken perhaps inappropriate steps to resolve the situation.

One final point to note in relation to crisis intervention is that we have to make sure that we receive adequate support ourselves. Sometimes, helping somebody through a major crisis in their life can place immense pressures on us. If we do not have adequate support systems in place, we run the risk of entering a crisis ourselves because the sometimes intense heat of the crisis moment can be too much for us to bear when added to our existing life pressures. Self-care is therefore an important part of capitalizing on crisis.

Practice focus 2.1

Kim had been struggling to deal with the conflicts in her team for some time and was beginning to wonder whether she would ever reach the point of having a team that pulled together instead of pulling apart. When it was announced that there would be a reorganization and her team might be disbanded, the team members were very shocked. To Kim's amazement, team members started to put their differences to one side and began to look at how they could campaign to retain their team identity in the new organizational structure.

Kim was able to capitalize on the crisis by getting the team to pull together to justify their existence in order to safeguard their future. She was delighted to see people who had been 'daggers drawn' previously were now working closely together in response to the crisis situation.

Chunk up or chunk down
Finding the right level of analysis

This rather strange-sounding tool comes from the world of neuro-linguistic programming (NLP). It has similarities with helicopter vision. According to this technique, there are two basic ways of focusing: broad and narrow. To switch from narrow to broad is referred to as chunking up; from broad to narrow as chunking down. To switch from big chunk thinking to small chunk thinking (chunking down), means moving away from the broad issues towards the finer detail. The opposite, chunking up, involves not getting bogged down in detail and trying to see how these details connect together to form a broader mosaic. It is not a question of deciding which is the 'correct' level of analysis, the broader issues versus the finer detail, but rather the ability and flexibility to switch between the two as appropriate.

Things can go wrong and our efforts can fail if we are looking at the wrong level at the wrong time. Part of the skill of high-quality people work is the ability to be able to recognize when it is appropriate to look at the broader issues and when it is appropriate to concentrate on the finer detail. It is not enough to focus on one at the expense of the other – we need the breadth of both. An approach that focuses on the wider issues, without concentrating on the significance of detail, can lead to disaster if one of those details happens to be crucial in determining the outcome of particular actions in a particular direction. Conversely, if we concentrate on details, we may not appreciate the way those details fit together into a significant pattern (as per 'Helicopter vision' below).

The ability to switch between the two levels and, just as importantly, to recognize when it is appropriate to do so, is an essential task of the people worker's repertoire. Sometimes we can be influenced by others in this regard. We may be working with someone, for example, who prefers to stick to the finer detail, who likes to have all the t's crossed and the i's dotted, and this can hold us back from looking at the broader picture. Alternatively, we may be working with somebody who is a big picture person, as it were, and who is reluctant to focus on precise detail, perhaps because there are particular details that he or she wishes to avoid (because they are painful, for example) or simply because that particular person finds it tedious to look at detail and is eager to remain at a broad level and trying to make progress without getting bogged down in detail. The trick, then, is getting the balance between the two. This is something that can be developed, over time, through experience and a focus on reflective practice – that is, analysing carefully how we tend to operate, making sure that we are switching between levels when we should be doing so. In other words, we are making every effort to learn from our experience and develop our skills in this particular area.

As with so many other tools, this one can be used at a number of different levels. For example, it can be used in working with teams. I have come across situations where certain teams tend to focus on the minutiae of particular issues. Particular concerns can dominate at the expense of looking at the overall situation. Sometimes these details are very important but if the team are not careful, they can be very destructive and counterproductive because the detail tends to obscure an understanding of the overall picture. By converse, it is also possible to have teams who, for example, hold meetings where they agree matters in broad outline, but do not discuss the detail of how this is going to be implemented. Consequently, it is quite possible that the agreement will never come to fruition because, although broad agreement was reached, nothing has happened to ensure that it is translated into specific action points that facilitate implementation. Both these problems – a focus on the smaller chunks and a focus on the bigger chunks – are unfortunately very common. A good people worker can be very helpful in supporting groups of staff in developing the flexibility necessary to switch between levels and not get stuck at either of them.

The CIA framework
Managing pressure and stress

This is a tool that is especially helpful in preventing stress from arising, or for helping people get out of difficult situations once stress has already managed to have become established in that particular set of circumstances. The CIA framework is an extension of development of the 'Serenity prayer', which suggests that we should change what we can change and accept what we cannot change. The CIA framework is a more sophisticated version of this.

C stands for control, **I** for influence and **A** for acceptance. The basic idea is that, in everything we do, there will be things that we can control, things that we cannot control but we can perhaps influence, and things that we can neither control nor influence and must ultimately accept. The theory behind the CIA framework is that if we do not assign the tasks we face to the appropriate category, then we are likely to experience unnecessary additional pressures that can lead to harmful stress. Let us look at each of the three elements in turn.

There is much in our life that we can control. However, if we do not control what is ultimately within our control, we run the risk of experiencing problems. An interesting and significant point to note here is that often the sphere of what we can control is much greater than people generally realize. People often feel uncomfortable about taking charge of particular issues and say 'I can't', when perhaps what they really mean is: 'I choose not to'. This can be very significant in people work from both sides of the fence, as it were. If the people we are seeking to help adopt this 'I can't' argument for things that they can actually control, then they will be closing off possible avenues of progress. They will be limiting themselves unnecessarily and perhaps thereby sustaining the problems they are experiencing. But for those of us involved in problem-solving work, failure to recognize what we can control can also be very problematic. It, too, can lead to avenues to progress being blocked off unnecessarily. We should therefore not be too hasty in deciding that certain things are beyond our control. If push came to shove, if we were really under pressure, could we actually control that particular thing? If we could control it in extreme circumstances, then why can't we control it in general circumstances? What is stopping us?

There are many things that we cannot control, but we can perhaps influence – other people, for example. Except for very extreme circumstances, one person cannot control the behaviour of another person, but it is a daily occurrence for people's behaviour to be influenced by the actions and attitudes of other people. We therefore need to ask ourselves, of those factors that are beyond my control, is there some way in which I can influence them? Again, there are two sides to this. We can help other people to look at what they can influence to change circumstances they are currently encountering, but we must also make sure that we practise what we preach in terms of looking at how we can influence the situations that we ourselves are part of. The point was made in Part One that there is a danger that problem solvers can become part of a culture of defeatism, cynicism and learned helplessness. Where such a culture exists, or even a tendency in that direction, it can result in things that can be influenced not being influenced because of this attitude of pessimism.

For those things that we cannot control, and we either cannot influence or have chosen not to influence for whatever reason (exhaustion after years of trying, for example), the only option then is acceptance. If we cannot control or influence a situation, then clearly we have to accept it. However, it may take time for people to come to terms with this. It can be similar to a process of grieving, to let go of our hopes of resolving a situation and accept that it is not going to change.

Pressure can be increased, perhaps resulting in harmful levels of stress where we are unsuccessful in assigning the challenges we face to the appropriate category of CIA. For example, if there are things that we can control, but fail to do so, then we can experience increased levels of pressure. If I am in control of communicating important information to a particular person, but do not do so, then I must accept the consequences of that, and this may well add to the pressures that I face. If there are things that I could influence, but do not attempt to, then, as indicated earlier, I am unnecessarily limiting myself and cutting off possible solutions. For example, if somebody's behaviour is causing me distress, but they are unaware of this, then my failure to raise the issue tactfully and assertively with them could lead to a vicious circle whereby my distress is increased, resulting in greater reluctance to address the issue, thus resulting in greater distress, and so on.

In terms of acceptance, this too can be problematic when people do not accept what ultimately they have to. Notwithstanding the transition period often required, as mentioned earlier, people can create a great deal of worry, anxiety and ill-feeling by becoming stuck in between, on the one hand, control and influence and, on the other, acceptance. That is, they are neither controlling nor influencing, but nor are they accepting. They may be raging against a particular set of circumstances and this can become a dangerous situation in which they are trapped in a cycle that generates aggression outwardly or turns inwards as depression. Sometimes, these issues can be so complex that particular individuals may need professional help in dealing with them. However, this does not alter the fact that most of us, most of the time, should be able to make sure that we:

- control what we can control;
- influence what we can influence; and
- accept those things that we can neither control nor influence.

Once again, this is a tool that can be used at different levels:

- as an individual, self-awareness, self-help tool;
- as a tool of intervention with others who are experiencing difficulty in managing their pressures; or
- as an exercise with a group.

It can also be used either in a preventative way, to make sure that problems do not arise in future, or in a remedial way to address problems that have already arisen.

The CIA framework was first introduced in my book, *Stress Matters*, in 1999. Since then, I have had many people tell me that adopting this framework has made a huge difference to their lives. By making sure that they control what they can control, this has given them a greater sense of confidence. In turn, that has given them greater confidence to try and influence what they cannot control and they have learned by becoming more skilled and confident at the control and influence levels to recognize what they have to accept.

Congruence
Getting on the same wavelength

A recurring theme across many of these tools is the need to 'engage' or connect with people. Unless we are able to do this effectively, it is unlikely we will be able to make a positive difference in relation to the problems they face (and/or they are causing). Congruence is a tool that can be used to help in this regard.

It has its roots in neuro-linguistic programming (NLP), although it can be used in its own right without having to make any commitment to this particular approach to interpersonal relations. The key to the NLP version of congruence, then, is being able to recognize the style of communication a person feels comfortable with and using that style with them, so that they feel more comfortable with you.

In NLP these styles of communication are linked to the senses. Basically there are three types, as follows:

- *Visual* A 'visual' person is likely to use language related to sight or vision, such as: 'I see what you mean', 'I get the picture', 'Do you see where I'm coming from?'
- *Auditory* An 'auditory' person is likely to use language related to hearing, such as: 'I hear what you're saying', 'That rings a bell', 'Sounds good to me'.
- *Feeling (or 'kinaesthetic')* 'I grasped the idea straight away', 'I just couldn't connect with what she was saying', 'It didn't feel right'.

The basic argument is that each of us will feel more comfortable with our 'favourite' style, although we will not be restricted to that style. That is, we may use a mixture of styles at any one time, but we are more likely, it is argued, to favour one style over the others.

To use congruence as a tool with a particular individual, we need to listen carefully to what he or she is saying and see whether we can note what style (visual, auditory or feeling) is featuring most. If we then adopt that particular style, we increase the chances of the individual concerned feeling comfortable with us (thereby increasing the chances of 'engagement' and being able to make progress in tackling whatever problems need our attention).

In my view, the NLP approach places too much emphasis on the sensory dimension of communication styles. While there may well be a case for arguing that sensory preferences play a part in shaping communication patterns, I feel that there are other dimensions of communication style that also need to be considered – for example, formality. Some people like to speak on a fairly formal basis and may feel they are not being taken seriously if we speak to them in too casual a style. Conversely, someone who feels more comfortable with informal styles of speech may feel alienated by formal speech on our part.

In addition to sensory differences, styles of communication can vary in the following ways:

> formal vs. informal
> direct vs. indirect
> open vs. closed
> telling vs. asking
> calm vs. aroused

and so on.

Communication is a very complex topic and it is dangerous to oversimplify it. However, it remains the case that there is much to be gained by developing congruence in our communication by (i) trying to find common ground (in terms of communication styles) with the person(s) we are seeking to help; and (ii) also matching the style of communication to the context in which we are working (for example, informal style in an interview that forms part of a formal investigation may not be appropriate).

To develop congruence as a tool you may find it helpful to think about your own preferred styles of communication and those of others you regularly interact with.

- Can you identify any patterns (sensory or otherwise)?
- Try to get into the habit of listening to other people's styles of communication. Can you recognize any patterns there?
- Who do you regard as a really good communicator? Does he or she use particular styles?
- When you encounter a conflict situation, are the antagonists using different styles of communication?

Over time you can develop a heightened awareness and increased sensitivity to communicative styles and thus be able to develop your skills in working with people in a variety of settings by making good use of congruence. If you work with someone on a short-term basis, it will be a big challenge (but not necessarily an impossible one) to be able to become sufficiently sensitive to their communication styles. However, if you work with someone over a longer period, you are likely to find it easier to identify their communication preferences.

A word of caution should be sounded here, though. Beware of making the mistake of equating congruence with matching. The NLP emphasis on sensory preferences implies that it is best to match the other person's style so that they feel comfortable with you. In many situations this will be highly appropriate. However, in others, a congruent style may actually be one that differs from the other person's. Congruent should be read as 'fitting' rather than 'matching', as in some circumstances, it is fitting to use an opposing style – for example, using an open style in working with someone who is adopting a closed style.

Congruence can be used on a one-to-one basis as an aid to communication – for example, when we are in discussion with a particular person. However, it can also be used in helping people relate to one another. For example, in work involving conflict (whether between two people or within a group), looking at communication styles could be a potentially useful way forward. If it is found that there are conflicting styles of communication, this could become the basis of trying to resolve any difficulties being experienced.

Consequences
Exploring options and their likely outcomes

This is a very simple tool that can be very effective in helping people appreciate where their behaviour is likely to lead them to. It can be used in circumstances where someone is behaving in a way that is causing problems, either for themselves or for other people. This can be for a variety of reasons. It may be that the individual concerned is deliberately being destructive (or self-destructive) or it may be that the emotional pressures of the situation have led to this individual behaving in problematic ways (for example, someone feeling stressed and taking it out on other people instead of trying to identify the cause of the stress and deal with it).

The technique involves taking a sheet of paper and drawing a line down the middle to form two columns. The left-hand side column should be headed 'Actions' and the right-hand side 'Consequences'. Through discussion with the individual concerned, a number of courses of action can be listed on the left-hand side. These should arise through discussion and should include both courses of action that the person concerned has already undertaken or is likely to undertake plus others, which in your view, may be more appropriate in the circumstances. Both of you can contribute to drawing up the list, but it is best if most if not all of the options are elicited from the person concerned (so that he or she takes maximum ownership of the process and its outcomes).

You may, if you wish, add bizarre or ridiculous courses of action just to add a note of fun and humour. However, I would not recommend that you do this until you have used the technique a few times and feel comfortable and confident with it. Even then, you will need to judge carefully whether humour is appropriate to the situation. Of course, humour can be an excellent tension reliever and a great help in forming good working relationships, but it can also be disastrous if used inappropriately (for example, if it gives the message to the person you are trying to help: 'I am not taking your problems seriously').

The object of the exercise is to identify the likely consequences of each course of action and to weigh up, on the basis of that consideration, which is the best way forward. So, for each course of action listed on the left-hand side of the page, the likely consequences should be discussed and recorded on the right-hand side of the page. This can be done, for example, by asking simple questions like: 'If you were to do this (referring to an item on the left-hand side of the page), what do you think the likely consequences would be?' The response is then recorded on the right-hand side of the page. You would then move on to the next item on the left and ask the same question. In this way, you will build up a list of possible actions (on the left-hand side of the page) and the likely consequences of each (on the right-hand side).

As a practical point, you should make sure that you leave plenty of space between entries on the left-hand side of the column because it is likely that you will need more space on the right-hand side for recording the consequences of the action concerned (although, by using note form, you should be able to overcome any problems here).

What should happen is that the individual concerned will co-operate in identifying likely problematic/harmful consequences of certain courses of action and more positive/constructive consequences of their actions. In other words, it should become apparent which courses of action have desirable consequences and which do not.

This process, then, involves weighing up the pros and cons of each particular course of action. This can be very useful in helping somebody to appreciate how what they have been doing, or what they are likely to do, can be harmful for themselves and/or for others. It is a helpful way of bringing order to what can perhaps be a chaotic, confused and complex situation. Consider the following example:

ACTION	CONSEQUENCE
Bite people's heads off.	I feel better in the short term, but worse overall. People like me less and I risk losing friends.
Say nothing and keep my anger to myself.	I don't risk losing friends, but I feel worse and I risk letting all the bad feelings bottle up until they all come rushing out at once. Or, I make myself ill by bottling it up.
Tell people calmly why I am not happy.	This would be great, but I'm not sure I could do it.
Avoid the problem in the first place before it builds up.	I would be much happier with this. I would not lose friends and I would stay calm and feel better. But I'm not sure I would know how to do this.

Here we have identified only four actions and sets of consequences, but could have taken this further. However, even with only four options to explore, a clear pattern is emerging: we are able to identify that this person could benefit from help with preventing pressures from building up and in keeping calm when they do. The exercise will also have taught him or her that biting people's heads off is not a helpful reaction and that alternative responses need to be developed.

One important note of caution, though, is that you should be careful not to make this a lesson in moralizing. It is very easy to oversimplify this process and to polarize good actions and bad actions. This can come across to the individual concerned as simplistic and unhelpful. As with any tool, it needs to be used with skill and care. When used appropriately, it can be helpful in identifying problems to be avoided and alternative courses of action. When not used appropriately, it can appear to be a club to beat somebody with. We have to be careful to make sure that we promote the former and avoid the latter.

This approach can be particularly helpful with children but, of course, it will be necessary to take into account their level of development and establish whether or not they will be sufficiently mature to understand the process and its outcomes.

Cost-benefit analysis
Balancing the pros and cons

This technique is a near relation to 'SWOT analysis' (to be discussed later), in so far as it has certain things in common. However, it is also different in significant ways. It is simpler than SWOT analysis, because it involves two elements rather than four, but it is also more complex than SWOT analysis, in so far as it explores those two elements in much more detail.

Cost-benefit analysis is basically a decision-making tool. It involves taking a sheet of paper, drawing a line down the centre, heading the left-hand column 'costs', and the right-hand column 'benefits'. When trying to make a decision about whether to adopt a particular course of action, this analysis can be very useful in giving us some very strong messages about what problems we might encounter or, indeed, how we might gain advantage by adopting that particular route. What can be particularly useful is to break down the costs into their different types. What types are applicable will depend on the circumstances but these can include:

- financial costs;
- human costs (will anyone suffer in some way if this decision is made?);
- goodwill costs (will this course of action cause ill-feeling?);

- opportunity costs (will we be closing other doors by opening this particular door?);
- reputation costs (will people think less of us if we adopt this plan?); and
- ethical costs (does this course of action compromise our values in any way?).

We can then adopt a similar process in terms of highlighting the benefits. These too can be broken down into their different types along much the same lines as the costs. Some people adopt a very mechanistic approach to cost-benefit analysis by, for example, attaching figures to costs and benefits, adding up the totals and then deciding how to proceed, based on the mathematical result from this. To my mind, this is too rigid an approach. It oversimplifies some very complex issues and is therefore best avoided.

Some people have a very narrow perspective on cost-benefit analysis. They may have used it in its literal sense – that is, at a financial level, to look at what benefits we will get for our money (the cost). However, this technique can be used much more widely and much more creatively to look at any situation because, if we think of costs and benefits in a much wider sense than purely financial, then this can be a useful tool for weighing up advantages and disadvantages, pluses and minuses.

One important consideration when developing a cost-benefit analysis is to look at: for whom is this a cost? And, for whom is it a benefit? If we do not do this, we may miss out on some key issues. For example, there may be conflicts between particular groups that may not come out unless we ask these important questions around this key issue of 'for whom?' Asking these questions may also indicate why certain people are resistant to change. It may well be that, from where they are sitting, there are lots of costs but few benefits. Other people may be very keen to adopt a particular course of action because, from their point of view, there are few costs but great benefits. We must therefore not oversimplify the issue by looking at cost and benefit in absolute terms but, rather, to make these issues relative to the positions of particular individuals or groups who have an interest in the outcome of the situation we are dealing with (stakeholders).

Cost-benefit analysis can be helpful for individuals to use as a means of weighing up options. It can be something that we can do with other people as a tool of intervention – for example, when somebody is so anxious about a situation that they are paralysed when it comes to decision making. Similarly, it can be used to help people who are rushing into a particular course of action without fully weighing up the consequences and finally, it can be used with groups of people for making joint decisions about particular courses of action. One bonus of using it in this way is that it can identify actual or potential conflicts between different stakeholders within that group.

Practice focus 2.2

Liam was faced with quite a challenge when trying to help Tom resolve his current difficulties. Tom had been through a period of major change and was now 'punch drunk', feeling very confused about what to do next and very anxious that, in this unsettled period in his life, he might make decisions that he might regret later. Liam asked Tom whether he had ever used cost-benefit analysis. Tom replied that he had heard of it but was not entirely sure what was involved in it. Once Liam explained, Tom was keen to pursue this. Liam therefore sat down with him, helped him identify the various options available to him and to weigh up the costs and benefits of each. Tom found this a very helpful process, especially as the structure it provided gave him a sense of security and boundaries, something that had been missing from his life recently because of all the changes he had been through.

Critical incident technique
Learning from significant experiences

This is a method that can be used by supervisors in trying to help their supervisees to learn from their experience. It involves the following steps:

1. Identify a particular incident which is significant in some way. It may have particular emotional connotations, or there may be other aspects of the situation that make it stand out from day-to-day practice.
2. Briefly record what happened in the incident. There is no need for a detailed description here, just the key points.

3. Record how you would account for what happened in this incident. In other words, provide a basic explanation for what occurred.
4. What other explanations could there be for what happened? For example, what other conceptual framework could help us to understand this incident?

This can be a very helpful way of encouraging practitioners to think carefully about what happens in their work and how they account for what happens. It can be very useful for linking theory to practice for helping practitioners (and indeed managers) to realize that their work is based on a professional knowledge base, even though this may not always be explicit. As I have commented previously:

> This simple but effective framework provides an excellent basis for discussion and exploration of the linkages between theory and practice in a way which enhances practice and brings theory to life. It is a technique which can be used on a one-to-one basis or as part of a group exercise.
>
> An important point to note, however, in using this technique is that it can often generate strong emotions. Incidents encountered can have a powerful emotional impact and the analysis of the incident can rekindle intense and painful feelings. This has two sets of implications:
>
> 1. Facilitators need to be ready and able to work constructively with such feelings as and when they arise, for example by creating a safe environment.
> 2. It needs to be remembered that theory has a role to play in dealing with the emotional dimension . . . We need to be wary of the false assumption that theory is 'rational', and therefore incompatible with the 'irrational' world of feelings.
>
> The use of the critical incident technique therefore represents an important and potentially very effective strategy for integrating theory and practice. (Thompson, 2000, pp. 100–1)

This is a well-established technique that has an associated literature. It can be very helpful in encouraging practitioners to think about their practice and to develop, from this, critically reflective approaches to practice. However, in a revised version, this technique can also be used to help people we are trying to support through problem situations to develop an awareness of their own part in what is happening to them – to develop insight into the situation they face.

This revised version would involve:

1. identifying an incident that has caused concern to the person concerned;
2. clarifying what happened in that incident;
3. seeking their explanation for what happened; and
4. looking at alternative explanations.

Once again, this is a tool that should be used with skill and craft and not simply in a mechanistic, unthinking way. If handled carefully and sensitively, it can help individuals to appreciate that their initial understanding of a situation may be misleading and that there are other explanations for what has happened. If we simply tell somebody that they are wrong and that they have misunderstood a situation, we should not be surprised if we meet resistance. If, however, we help them to explore alternative explanations, then they may well come to the conclusion themselves that their initial view was a partial one and needs to be replaced by an alternative version. This is not to say that people's understanding of their problems will always be misguided or inaccurate or partial, but we have to be realistic and recognize that this is often the case. We should not be surprised by this, as it is often the result of the tensions associated with the problem situation. It is not uncommon for people facing significant problems to find it difficult to think clearly, or to adopt a balanced overview of the situation.

The technique can also be used as a team-building exercise or, indeed, with any group of people who need to look at particular events and explore their understanding of them. This four-step process can give a clear and helpful framework that provides structure and focus for a skilled facilitator to use to enable the group of people concerned to broaden their understanding, deepen their insight and look at positive ways forward.

Doing the right things vs. doing things right
Balancing efficiency and effectiveness

The distinction between doing the right things and doing things right is generally associated with the management thinker, Peter

Drucker (see Drucker, 1954). It is broadly similar to the distinction between effectiveness and efficiency (effectiveness = doing the right things, efficiency = doing things right). Being effective means achieving our goals. Being efficient means achieving those goals with the most effective use of the resources available to us – that is, without waste.

Sometimes we can be effective in that we achieve our goals, but it is not necessarily the case that we do so efficiently. That is, while we may well achieve our goals, we may do so in a way that involves greater use of resources than was necessary. Such resources could be physical, financial or human. Ironically, it is possible for us to be efficient without being effective – that is, we may be concentrating on making sure that we do not waste resources and make the best use of the resources available to us, but without necessarily achieving our goals. This can be linked to the discussion of systematic practice in Part One of the book, where it was emphasized that it is important to keep a clear focus on what we are trying to achieve. It is sadly the case that the history of organizational life is littered with examples of teams of staff, or even whole organizations, who have devoted considerable time and effort to making sure that they were operating efficiently, but without making sure that they were actually achieving their goals. This results in a bizarre situation where efforts to save time and money through efficiency end up being perhaps a total waste of time and money, because all the resources invested in that effort do not achieve the goals that they are intended to. This can happen for a variety of reasons. One very common one is that people get engrossed in 'office politics' and lose sight of the reasons for their organization's existence or the specific aims it is trying to achieve.

The worst case scenario is when our efforts are neither effective nor efficient. That is, we fail to achieve what we set out to do and use up a great deal of resources in the process. Sadly, this is not uncommon. We could devote a whole book to the possible reasons for this but, for present purposes, suffice it to say that the complex organizational and interpersonal dynamics involved in people work can often result in this worst case outcome.

The best case scenario is, of course, the direct opposite of the above. This is where we are both effective and efficient. That is, we both achieve our aims and do so with the best use of the resources available to us. While it would certainly be idealistic to expect to achieve this every time, we should be working towards achieving this best case scenario as frequently as we possibly can.

An important way of doing this is to keep a clear focus on both aspects – the efficiency and the effectiveness. That is, to make sure that we are doing the right things and that we are doing them right. A necessary prerequisite for this is reflective practice, as discussed in Part One. It is important that we allow ourselves the space to be able to review what we are doing and to plan ahead. If we allow ourselves to fall into the trap of rushing around trying to achieve too much, then the danger is that we may achieve very little and waste a lot of time, effort, energy and money (not to mention the good will of others) in the process.

Systematic practice can help us to make sure that we are doing the right things, that we have a clear picture of our objectives and how we are intending to meet them (and, of course, how we will know when we have met them). To this we need to add the dimension of efficiency to make sure that we are 'doing things right'. This can be achieved by exploring the various options available to us and not simply relying on the first thing that comes to mind. This is because, while the first thing that comes to mind may well work (although even that is not guaranteed), it may well be the case that there are other methods that could be equally successful, if not more so, but which involve less use of valuable resources.

To sum up, what this important technique involves is:

1. being clear about what we are trying to achieve (as per systematic practice – the S of PRECISE practice);
2. exploring different options for achieving those ends;
3. seeking to ensure that the option we have chosen is, where appropriate, the most efficient as well as most effective; and
4. ensuring that we do not allow a narrow-minded focus on efficiency to mean that we are not being effective, thus leading to a significant waste of resources. We should make every effort to ensure that this 'fool's efficiency' is not allowed to hijack our efforts to achieve effectiveness.

The drama triangle
Avoiding being drawn into being a 'rescuer'

This is a framework associated with transactional analysis. It warns of the dangers of getting drawn inappropriately into conflict situations. It can be a useful tool to clarify your own thinking and also help others (individuals or groups) to understand the problems they are experiencing.

In the drama triangle, there are three players. First, we have an individual who feels that someone else is giving him or her a hard time. This is the person known as the victim. The person in the 'victim' role is someone who feels that another person is acting unfairly or is even deliberately 'gunning for' him or her. The role of victim can be real or imagined. That is, the victim's perception may be based in objective reality or not, but if the person occupying the victim role perceives him- or herself as a victim, then he or she will act accordingly. We therefore have to take this seriously, even if there is no objective basis to that perception.

The second player in the drama triangle is the person referred to as the persecutor. The person occupying this role may not perceive him- or herself as a persecutor but, if perceived as such by the 'victim', then the unhealthy dynamic between victim and persecutor can none the less commence. In many situations the dynamic can be reciprocated – that is, one person perceives the other as a persecutor, while that person perceives the so-called victim as a persecutor – each feels that the other is being difficult. This is a common occurrence in negotiation situations or, indeed, in conflict situations more broadly. It is a very unhelpful dynamic, whether one-way or reciprocal, because what it tends to do is to 'lock' each person into that particular role, to encourage them to become entrenched in their respective views. He or she then fails to see the broader picture and tends to see the situation only from that specific role definition, whether it is accurate or not.

If the perception of role is accurate, it can be a significant problem, as the individual concerned will tend to adopt a narrow perspective and is likely to fail to see the big picture (see the discussion of 'Helicopter vision' below). Where the perception is inaccurate, for whatever reason, then this can make the situation even worse, as it means that this particular individual is adopting a distorted perception. One of the things that the drama triangle teaches us is that one person's distorted perception can lead to distorted perceptions on the part of others. It can be a destructive dynamic in this respect. For example, a victim's attitude towards their alleged persecutor can lead the persecutor to feel guilty, even though he or she may have done nothing wrong.

The third player in the drama triangle is known as the rescuer. Professional helpers can often be cast in the role of rescuer. People involved in the destructive victim–persecutor dynamic, especially the person occupying the victim role, can put great pressure on problem solvers to adopt the rescuer role, to come to their aid in removing them from the situation of being persecuted. Being drawn into the rescuer role is a very dangerous move for a problem solver. A very easy mistake to make is to be seduced by the victim's claims of being persecuted to the point where we fall into the trap of seeking to rescue the victim from the 'evil' persecutor. Where this happens we have, in effect, been seduced into taking sides in a conflict situation and/or played a part in reinforcing an individual's distorted perception of how they are being treated by another person or persons. This can be disastrous. We can find that our efforts to help have actually made the situation worse (see Practice focus 2.3). What can be particularly destructive about the drama triangle when we get drawn into it is that it can prevent us from adhering to the principles of good practice. For example, it can lead us to miss out the assessment stage and move straight into trying to resolve a problem without first looking at the precise nature of the problem, the factors relevant to it, and so on.

An important stance to take when faced with the situation that could lead us into the drama triangle is to remember to remain neutral. These situations are often based on conflicts and, in any conflict situation, it can be dangerous to take one side against the other without first carefully weighing up the situation and considering our role within it. Before we act on one person's perception of the situation, we need to check out the perceptions of others involved, so that we can get an overview and make up our own mind about how best to intervene (if at all).

What makes a drama triangle particularly dangerous is that people involved in people problem solving are often highly motivated to resolve difficulties and to assist people in distress. The plea of the victim can therefore be very seductive and draw us into this destructive three-way interaction by bypassing our normal practices such as assessment, gaining an overview of the situation, checking our perceptions with others, and so on. That is, problem solvers are particularly prone to being drawn into this triangle. We therefore have to be very wary of it.

Practice focus 2.3

Diane had been aware of conflicts between Paul and Graham for some time. However, she was very surprised when Paul came to her and claimed that Graham had been bullying him. Paul was quite distressed and was making strong allegations against Graham. Diane was very supportive of Paul and promised that she would help him deal with Graham's inappropriate behaviour, if necessary through disciplinary proceedings. After Paul left, she was quite annoyed at Graham and she felt that, although he and Paul had never got on, he had gone too far this time. She decided she would need to take a firm line in dealing with him.

She was therefore very surprised indeed when, later that afternoon, Graham came to see her to seek her support in making a complaint about Paul's behaviour. He claimed that Paul had been intimidating him and had threatened to 'get him into trouble'. Diane was taken aback by this and had to review her understanding of the situation. Who was the victim here and who was the persecutor? She realised that it wasn't that simple and that she had made the mistake of forming a view of the situation having heard only one side of the story. She didn't know who to believe but she did know that she had made a mistake in allowing herself to be drawn into a drama triangle situation and that she would need to assess the situation more carefully before deciding what to do about it.

Eating an elephant
Being realistic about what we can achieve

This refers to the old but important question of 'How do you eat an elephant?' and the equally important reply of 'One mouthful at a time'. What this tool is about is ensuring that we do not bite off more than we can chew. What it is concerned with can be summed up in one short phrase: reasonable ambition. This is to be contrasted with the two unhelpful extremes of:

1. A lack of ambition where people are defeatist and render themselves helpless and powerless, perhaps unnecessarily so. This lack of confidence and ambition can be a major drawback in trying to deal with many problems.
2. At the other extreme, we can have too much ambition. Being overambitious can, in certain circumstances, be disastrous. It can lead to lots of effort and energy being wasted when our efforts have collapsed as a result of our taking too much on and then finding that we cannot cope with the pressures.

In between these two extremes of lack of ambition and overambition, is the healthy balance of realistic ambition, as I like to call it. Realistic or reasonable ambition is about being sensible about how much we can reasonably take on. An important issue here is self-awareness. Think for a moment about your own tendencies (or ask somebody who knows you well). Which is more likely if you are going to get it wrong? Are you likely to be not ambitious enough (not fulfilling your potential) or too ambitious (taking on more than you can cope with)? The answer to this question will give you a strong clue as to how to proceed in terms of making sure you achieve the balance of being realistically ambitious. If you have a tendency to lack ambition, then this raises issues of confidence. If you have the opposite tendency, namely to be overambitious, then this is giving you a warning shot across the bows, as it were, and telling you that you need to focus on being realistic.

Whichever direction you tend to go in (if either), the tool of eating an elephant can be very helpful. The basic message of 'How do you eat an elephant?' is that it is important to break large projects down into manageable chunks or 'bite-size pieces'. Taking on a large project can be a significant undertaking. People who tend to be not ambitious enough can find it so daunting that they may choose not to get involved at all and thus miss some valuable opportunities for progress and development. People who are overambitious may try to tackle things too hastily. In either case, breaking the project down into its component parts can be a very valuable and worthwhile exercise. In fact, it is often essential for success.

An important way of doing this is to get the overview of the project, the big picture, as it were (see the discussion of 'Helicopter vision' below). By having such an overview, you should be able to break it down into its main sections. If those sections are manageable as they stand, then this should be sufficient. However, depending on the size of the project, these sections may also need to be divided into subsections. This can be achieved by drawing a tree diagram – see the discussion below of using 'Objectives trees'.

The 'eating an elephant' technique can be used in two ways. First, you can use it yourself as a guide to managing your own projects. It can be very helpful in making sure that you do not get yourself into difficulties in terms of large projects. Second, it can also be used as a tool for helping others, those you are seeking to help (whether individuals or groups). You can help other people to become more proficient in managing their projects by supporting them in achieving the reasonable ambition that is part and parcel of the notion of 'eating an elephant'. For example, managers can help the staff they supervise to make sure that they are operating according to this principle, while staff in the caring professions may find that the people they are seeking to help are having difficulties because they are either biting off more than they can chew or are not having the confidence to tackle the issues they can tackle because they perceive the overall challenge ahead of them as being too big.

Eco maps
Mapping out relationships across groups of people

An eco map is a tool deriving from an 'ecological' approach to working with people – that is, one that emphasizes the relationship between the individual and his or her environment. It is helpful in moving away from individualistic models that focus too narrowly on individuals and do not take sufficient account of wider factors in the individual's environment that may also be significant.

Different people draw eco maps in different ways, and so there is no standardized way of doing so. Figure 2.1 provides an example of one way of producing such a map. What they will tend to have in common is a means of mapping relationships between an individual and key aspects of his or her environment, including people and organizations.

They can be used in different ways: a means of clarifying our own thinking about a particular situation; a tool for helping people understand their own situation; or a method of helping members of a group or team to understand and, where necessary, change group dynamics. Let us consider each of these in turn.

In trying to help someone without falling into the trap of failing to take account of important environmental or contextual factors, we can make good use of an eco map. We place the individual concerned at the centre of the map, then consider the significant people, organizations or factors that are impinging on the situation we are dealing with and represent these on the map. Next we can draw the connections or relationships between the individual and the contextual factors as a set of lines. We can use different types of lines (or different colours) to indicate different types of relationship. Commonly used are:

- *weak vs. strong (or distant vs. close)*   This gives us an indication of how significant the relationship is.
- *positive vs. negative*   Is it a helpful or a problematic relationship?
- *formal vs. informal*   For example, formal line management vs. informal mentoring relationship.
- *direction of power*   This maps out power relationships.

However, these are not the only ones that can be used. Indeed, you are free to use whatever suits your particular purpose at the time.

Once we have completed the map, we can then look at it closely to see if anything significant strikes us about the set of relationships

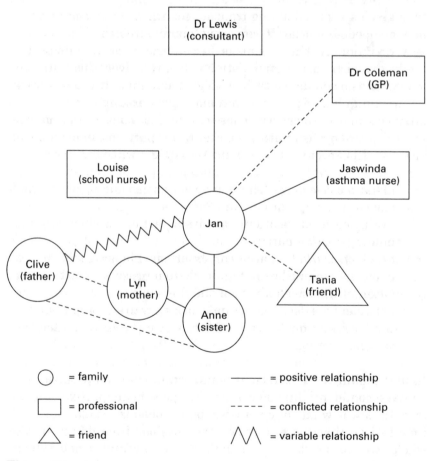

Figure 2.1   An eco map

we have identified. It is interesting how important patterns can emerge that may not have occurred to us otherwise – indeed, this is the major strength of an eco map as a tool for clarifying our thinking about a situation. Note, though, that the use of an eco map for clarifying our own thinking should not lead us into adopting a course of action without first consulting and involving the person we are trying to help (see the discussion of partnership in Part One).

We can go through the same process of drawing up an eco map jointly with the person we are trying to help, so that they have an important input into the process. Their perception of the situation may be very different from our own – and this may tell us a lot about the circumstances we are dealing with. Even where their perception matches ours closely, the exercise can be a very useful one in presenting a picture of the relationships involved. It can then give us a good starting point for identifying any changes that may be needed in order to solve or alleviate problems.

A variation on this theme is to ask the person concerned to produce their own eco map (after you have given them suitable instructions or guidance on how to go about this). If you are working with a group of people or a team, each person can be asked to produce a map of their own. These can then be collated (perhaps by an independent facilitator) to see what patterns emerge. This process will generally produce two sets of factors to consider:

- *areas of consensus* This can be very significant – to establish clearly what group or team members seem to agree on (for example, that a relationship with a particular external stakeholder is problematic).
- *areas of conflict* There can be areas of disagreement that emerge which will need to be tackled if progress is to be made. Often conflicts remain beneath the surface and have a very detrimental effect unless and until they are brought out into the open and dealt with – the eco map process can facilitate that happening.

In undertaking this exercise it is important that you promise (and deliver) confidentiality. For example, people are unlikely to be truthful about what they perceive as a problematic relationship if they believe that there may be repercussions from doing so. The whole process needs to be handled carefully and sensitively to ensure that it does not cause any unnecessary complications.

A team or group of people could also be asked to develop an eco map as a group exercise. That is, rather than collating individual maps from team members, your role could be to facilitate a group or team eco map – on a sheet of flip chart paper, for example.

Congress (2002) argues that eco maps do not take enough account of cultural diversity. She proposes a 'culturagram' as an alternative to, or development of, an eco map. However, my view is that a separate approach is not needed. If we are taking equality and diversity issues seriously then we should be incorporating such issues into all our actions and should not need a separate tool for doing so. The 'environment' should be interpreted widely to include contextual factors of a sociological as well as psychological nature, including class, gender and race and culture.

Eco maps offer useful insights into complex interrelationships. By mapping out how the individual relates to aspects of his or her environment (and aspects of the environment can relate to each other), we can develop useful pictures that help to deepen our understanding and provide a basis for planning and implementing change.

Elegant challenging
Being constructive in challenging unacceptable
behaviour or language

The problems we encounter as people workers are often character-ized by conflict. Sometimes that conflict arises because a particular person is behaving or speaking in a way that others object to. For example, somebody may be prone to making racist or sexist comments. This can create a lot of tension and ill feeling. Unfortunately, such situations are often not handled very well. This is because, as Figure 2.2 shows, individuals can go to one unhelpful extreme or the other, and often do not find the healthy balance in between.

One unhelpful extreme is simply to ignore what has been said or done, to pretend that it has not been noticed. This can be very problematic because, in effect, it colludes with the racism, sexism or whatever form of discrimination that is being expressed. People who make such comments are likely to be encouraged to continue making them if no one raises any objections. He or she could

| Collusion/ not challenging | Elegant challenging | Aggressive challenging |

Figure 2.2 Elegant challenging

understandably assume that it is acceptable to make such comments, given that no protest is expressed. At the other extreme, which can be equally harmful, we can have a very strong, even aggressive reaction. This is often problematic because, for one thing, it tends to increase tensions, rather than decrease them and, for another, it creates a situation where the individual who has behaved inappropriately becomes defensive. In such circum-stances, he or she is likely to see the problem as being the overre-action of the other party, rather than the inappropriateness of their own behaviour or language. This strong reaction therefore gives the individual concerned a way out of the situation. It enables him or her to reframe the situation as one of overreaction rather than inappropriate action on their part.

In between these two extremes is what is known as elegant chal-lenging. Elegant means sophisticated, and so an elegant challenge is one that is not crude or ill-thought through. It is where the person doing the challenging raises the issue in a helpful way, rather than in an aggressive or attacking way. This can involve using assertiveness skills: finding ways of making it clear to the person concerned that their actions are not acceptable, but doing so in a subtle and constructive way, rather than a personal attack. This is built on the assertiveness principle that if you are reason-able, it puts pressure on the other party to be equally reasonable. However, if your response is excessive, then you are not encourag-ing the other party to be reasonable, but rather reinforcing an ethos of unreasonableness.

This tool can be used in the workplace – for example, where you may have a colleague whose behaviour is causing problems and needs to be tackled carefully and sensitively. However, it can also be used as a tool of intervention in helping people solve their prob-lems. If, for example, one individual is behaving in a way that causes problems for others, you may find that other people's response is at one of the destructive extremes. That is, they may not acknowledge that it is a problem and so it continues to fester, as it were, or they may go to the other extreme and up the tension by reacting in an aggressive manner, thus causing problems of interpersonal relations. Helping people to challenge elegantly, to find ways of broaching difficult subjects in constructive and supportive ways, can be a very important way forward.

This can be a useful tool in a management setting – for example, in tackling a difficult appraisal issue where it is necessary to give somebody negative feedback about their performance (see the discussion of 'Giving feedback' below). There are ways and means of presenting issues of poor performance in a constructive and helpful light – in effect, an elegant challenge to seek to end the poor performance. This should, as indicated, avoid the destructive extremes of either not mentioning the issue (thus playing a part in perpetuating poor performance) or presenting the issue in a threatening or over the top way, which is likely to produce a defensive, and thus unhelpful reaction.

Elegant challenging is a very skilful technique. However, with practice, it can be honed to a state where it can be a very valuable tool indeed in our toolbox. It can be of immense benefit if used skilfully in the appropriate circumstances.

Practice focus 2.4

Laura was very anxious about taking up her job as a clerical assistant. It was her first job after leaving school and she was eager to make a good impression. On the first day she arrived smartly dressed and looking very attractive. Not long after she arrived in the office, she was spotted by a man who had a deserved reputation for making sexist remarks. When he saw her, he said: 'Oh look at that! I wouldn't mind getting her into bed'. When Laura heard this, she was very distressed. She was already feeling anxious and insecure and she had never been treated in this way by anyone before. She just wanted the floor to open up and swallow her, such was her embarrassment and distress. The staff who were present were furious with him for this and were tempted to 'go for the jugular'. However, instead, one of them, Sue, said to him: 'Oh come on, you can't say that. How would you feel if you had a teenage daughter and, on her first day in a new job, when she's very nervous and very keen to make a good impression, she had a middle-aged man leching over her and talking about getting her into bed? Would you think that was OK?' As it turned out, he did have a teenage daughter and, while this elegant challenge did not change his sexist attitudes overnight, it did make him think. Sue recognized that it certainly had a lot more impact than an angry response would have done, as this would simply have reinforced his view that the women in the office 'couldn't take a joke' without getting upset.

Embedded whys
Establishing reasons for our actions

In Part One I made reference to 'problem embedding' and likened it to Russian dolls where one is embedded in another. The same logic can be applied to the question, 'Why?' That is, often when we ask, 'Why?' we do not get a satisfactory answer and we then have to ask 'Why?' again, and perhaps another time or two as well. Larrick and Klayman (1998) capture this point well when they argue that:

> Workers at Toyota learned to ask 'Why?' five times before they generated hypotheses to solve a problem. When they did so, they were more likely to find a root cause rather than a superficial one. For example: (1) *Why did the machine stop?* Because the fuse blew due to an overload. (2) *Why was there an overload?* Because the bearing lubrication was inadequate. (3) *Why was the bearing lubrication inadequate?* Because the lubrication pump was not functioning properly . . . and so on. (p. 33)

The example given here is a mechanical one, but it should not take too much imagination to see how this technique can be applied to people and people problem solving.

But why should we want to ask, 'Why?' anyway? Well, basically, because asking 'Why?' can help us to understand the underlying reasons for problems. Sometimes we do not need to know the cause of a problem in order to solve it or at least alleviate it. For example, if somebody is starving, the problem can be solved by giving them food. We do not have to know why they were starving to offer them food. However, more often than not, it does pay to understand where a problem is coming from, as that is likely to give us a better indication of how to deal with it.

A common example of this is how we deal with stress. Some managers, when noticing that one of their staff is showing signs of stress, may suggest that they take a holiday. However, if the stress is being caused by having an excessive workload, being away from work on a holiday could actually make the problem worse. It can therefore sometimes be dangerous to try to solve problems without knowing more about what lies beneath them. This is where 'Why?' comes in, especially 'embedded whys'. Larrick and Klayman again offer apt comment when they argue that:

> In general, when individuals ask 'why' the first time, they are likely to develop answers that invoke some recent event. Subsequent 'whys' are likely to cause individuals to think more deeply about underlying problems that may recur. (p. 33)

The use of embedded whys can therefore help us get beneath the surface and start to see underlying factors that may need to be addressed in order to solve the problems we are trying to tackle.

Many people will have been taught, in counselling training, for example, that they should not ask 'Why?', but rather ask 'How?' The reason given for this proposed switch is normally that 'how?' is a less threatening question than 'why?' This may well be the case, but it is also a very different question from 'why?' – it will elicit a different response, and not necessarily the one we want in order to make progress. Rather than abandon asking 'why?' because some people may find it threatening, I believe it is far better to make sure that our use of this tool does not come across as threatening. The following pointers can be helpful in this regard:

- *Set out your stall* At the beginning of your working relationship make it clear that part of what you will do to try and be helpful will be to ask questions and often those questions will begin with 'Why?' Establish that you are doing this in order to develop a good understanding of the situation and that you are not trying to catch anyone out.
- *Ask it often* If you ask 'Why?' only occasionally, then it may come across as much more of an issue than if you are asking it on a fairly regular basis. If the people you are working with come to expect that you will ask why, they will be less bothered by this.
- *Use appropriate tone and body language* When asking why, make sure your tone of voice does not come across as threatening or intrusive. Similarly, your body language should be

giving a very clear non-threatening message. You may find it helpful to practise saying 'why' in different tones and noting how different the impact could be. You may also find it helpful to think about (or, better still, practise) what non-threatening body language would look like.

- *Use sentences*   Often 'Why?' on its own can be quite stark, but is far less harsh when part of a sentence. Consider, for example, a situation where someone says: 'I was so wound up that I felt I would want to kill the next person who annoyed me'. If the response is a simple 'Why?', that may come across as harsh and unsympathetic, but a full sentence, such as: 'Why did you feel like that?' comes across as far more responsive and supportive.
- *Encourage others to use 'Why'*   Make it clear that it cuts both ways, that you welcome other people asking you 'Why?'

There is no guarantee that people will always feel comfortable with being asked 'Why?', even when it is done with great skill and empathy. However, there are two important points to note here. First, by asking 'why?' skilfully and sensitively, rather than mechanistically, you are significantly increasing the chances of being able to help this person tackle their problems. Second, if they do find being asked 'why?' (in a skilful and sensitive manner) threatening, then that may well tell us something significant about their situation – for example, about their level of anxiety.

The empty chair
Exploring the influence of an absent person

––––––––––––

The empty chair technique is one that has long been used in family therapy, but can also be used to very good effect outside that context. Indeed, it has the potential to be used in a wide range of contexts or settings. It is used to try and understand somebody else's perspective and how particular people feel about that perspective. It can be especially useful in creating an atmosphere where people feel able to talk openly without fear of causing conflict or ill feeling.

The technique can be used in one of two basic ways, literally or metaphorically. When it is used literally, it involves having an empty chair physically present in the room. If somebody who is present is very angry towards someone who is not there, they can be asked to express their anger towards the empty chair, as if the person they are angry with were sitting in it. This may seem a bit silly, but it is surprising how effective it can be and how quickly people can adjust to talking to an empty chair. People may be more willing to say things to an empty chair that they feel too inhibited to say directly to the person concerned.

It is not only expressing anger that can be part of this process. Indeed, it can be used to express any feelings at all, and as such is a very good way of helping people vent what otherwise might remain as pent-up feelings. In this respect, it can be a very useful tool for encouraging people to talk openly about their feelings so that they can then be helped to deal with them (and/or deal with the situation that is causing them). For example, they can be helped to explore ways of communicating their feelings in a constructive way.

After someone has spoken to the empty chair, they can be asked 'What would he or she say in response if they were sitting in that chair?' This can help to develop a discussion further, again to iden-tify issues that need to be addressed. The use of the technique can also involve asking 'Why haven't you said this to him or her before? What has prevented you?' This can identify obstacles to communication, and it may well be an important part of helping this person to look at ways of removing or bypassing such obsta-cles. It can also help the person concerned to make the effort to try and understand the other person's point of view – to see both sides of the situation.

While literally using an empty chair can be a very powerful and effective use of symbolism, there is the downside that, as I suggested above, some people may feel it is a bit silly and may therefore feel too uncomfortable to benefit from it (or indeed, an inexperienced helper may not feel confident enough to carry it through). In such cases the alternative is to use the technique in a metaphorical way, rather than literally to have an empty chair present. This involves, asking questions like: 'If Tom were here now and asked you to speak openly about how you felt, what would you say to him?' or 'You are clearly feeling let down about how Lyn has treated you. Imagine I'm Lyn sitting here right now. What would you want to say to me? Don't hold back, just speak your mind.'

The examples I have given so far have involved using this technique with an individual. However, it can also be used in groups – for example, if you have a group of staff who are dissatisfied with a manager and there is some sort of investigation into the situation (perhaps the manager has been suspended as a result of allegations of bullying).

Of course, this technique has to be handled very carefully, as it can be very powerful and therefore potentially destructive if not handled appropriately. This is not one to be used lightly or without careful consideration of whether these circumstances are appropriate. If you are not an experienced people worker, but you feel this technique would be appropriate in a particular context, it may be worth considering whether it is worth enlisting the support of one or more experienced colleagues to undertake this work with you until you are more experienced and feel comfortable in using this powerful tool.

An important aspect of this technique to consider is its role in 'catharsis' (see the discussion of 'Recognizing grief' below). The technique can free up feelings that have been 'locked in' for some considerable time. This, in itself, can have positive benefits, but it can also be of considerable use in helping to identify positive ways forward. You need to be prepared for this, as the emotional outpourings can be quite significant. You may also want to make sure that the person going through this cathartic experience has somebody they know and trust to offer them emotional support in the immediate aftermath. They may feel the need to talk things through and you may not be available. In particularly emotionally charged circumstances, you may wish to make sure that the person you are working with has this moral support in place before you make use of the empty chair technique. It would also be wise to make sure that you have suitable support in place too, as an intensive outpouring of emotion can at times leave you feeling in need of an understanding person with a good listening ear.

Force-field analysis
Managing change

It is often said that the only thing that is constant is that we live and work in constantly changing circumstances. Change is said to be the norm. Force-field analysis is a very well-established technique, dating back to Kurt Lewin's work in 1947, that can be used as a useful way of looking at change. It can be used in a variety of ways, not least the following:

1. a planning or preparation tool (to be used before change in order to try and influence it or channel it in a particular direction – or indeed to attempt to prevent it, if it is an unwelcome change);
2. a problem-solving tool to work out why change is not working (to be used during a change process); or
3. to evaluate how change happened (after the change has occurred).

Given that so much of problem solving involves either promoting change or reacting to it, a tool geared towards managing change can be a very useful one in the problem solver's repertoire.

Force-field analysis involves identifying two sets of factors or 'forces'. These can include people, events, tendencies (aspects of a culture, for example) or anything else that can influence change (either by promoting it or by inhibiting it):

- *Driving forces* Those factors that destabilise the status quo and make change more likely – in other words, those aspects of the situation that push in the direction of change.
- *Restraining forces* These are 'inhibitory' forces, the factors that make change less likely. They are issues that will need to be overcome or bypassed if change is to take place.

This can be done in diagrammatic form, as indicated in Figure 2.3.

The technique can be used as a 'thinking tool'. That is, we can use it to clarify our own thinking. This can be of particular value in times of change (or where change is due to take place). Similarly, we can help others to clarify their thinking in times of change and uncertainty. In this way, it can be used to reduce anxiety and remove or reduce confusion – something that can be very useful in our problem-solving endeavours. And, of course, it can be used in group or team situations as a way of trying to prepare for change, handle it to best effect while it is happening and make sense of it and/or evaluate it after the event.

In addition to these three contexts (self, self and others and

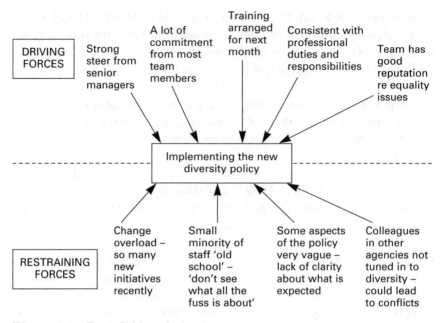

Figure 2.3 Force-field analysis

group/team), there are three sets of activities the tool can be used to support:

- *To promote change where it is needed* This would apply in situations where change is desirable – for example, where there is an unacceptable level of risk.
- *To maximize the positive potential of change* This relates to situations where change is happening anyway, but we are seeking to channel it in a particular direction so that we get the most benefit we can from the changing circumstances (see the discussion of 'Capitalizing on crisis' above).
- *To prevent change* It will often be the case that our problem-solving efforts are geared towards preventing deterioration in a situation and/or guarding against the harmful or destructive effects of change.

Some people seem to have a very rosy view of change and can become overzealous in promoting it. They seem to assume that change is necessarily progress or improvement and take little or no account of the costs of change and its potentially destructive impact. Force-field analysis can be useful in countering that naïve tendency, particularly if we use it in conjunction with other tools, such as 'SWOT analysis' and/or 'Cost-benefit analysis'.

Change is a central part of human experience, and so, as 'people workers' trying to solve human problems, we have to be very tuned in to change – its causes, its effects, its benefits and its costs. Force-field analysis does not do all that for us, but it does give us a very useful tool for moving in the right direction.

Giving feedback
Letting people know where they stand

When people are experiencing difficulties they can become very engrossed in what is going on around them and perhaps lose sight of their own part in the situation. To help with promoting problem solving we will often be called upon to give feedback to another person about their own behaviour or attitudes – and sometimes they will not necessarily want to hear what we have to say. For example, someone may be making their problems worse in how they are reacting to them. To make progress in dealing with the problems, it may be necessary to give the person concerned feedback about how they are dealing with the situation. This is a skilful and challenging job, as some people can react quite badly to being given feedback, even when it is done constructively and supportively as part of an attempt to help them deal with their problems.

Managers and supervisors in particular are likely to find that giving feedback – positive and negative – is an important part of their role. However, all of us involved in people work, whether managers or not, are likely to be required to give feedback at some time. It is therefore important to consider how best to do this in order to lay the foundations for developing good practice.

The skills involved in giving feedback can be developed to quite a high level but, for present purposes, we will need to be less ambitious and settle for covering the basics. The following pointers (taken from Gilbert and Thompson, 2002) should give you a good start in developing your skills in this area:

- *Be clear about what you are saying – don't fudge the issue* It is important that we should not allow our own anxiety to lead us into making a mess of giving feedback. If we are not clear about what we are trying to say, we will not communicate clearly and, if we do not communicate clearly, we run the risk of making the situation more tense and difficult than it needs to be. Therefore, it is essential that we (i) plan what we are going to say before we say it; and (ii) say it clearly. Fudging the issue will only make people nervous, and that can be a significant obstacle to progress.

- *Give balanced feedback – positives and negatives* Some people feel comfortable giving positive feedback (see the discussion of 'Positive strokes' below), but uncomfortable giving negative feedback, while for others it may be the reverse (some people feel they are being patronizing when they give positive feedback). Yet other people feel uncomfortable with both types of feedback, positive and negative! It is therefore important to develop your knowledge and skills over time to the point where you can feel reasonably comfortable with, and competent in, both sides of the feedback coin – positive and negative.

- *Raise concerns but don't make accusations* In trying to help people solve problems, you are entitled to give them feedback as you see fit, if this is geared towards making progress. However, if they feel they are being criticized, they might feel that you are accusing them of wrongdoing or incompetence. We should therefore be very careful to make sure that we do not say anything that could be interpreted as accusatory. This reinforces the point made above about being clear about what we are going to say before we say it.

- *Be prepared to listen – you may have got it wrong* We live and work in complex circumstances. It is very easy for things to be misunderstood, distorted or misrepresented, so we should not assume that the opinion we have formed is necessarily correct. We may have been misinformed or may have misinterpreted the situation (perhaps because of a key bit of information we were not aware of at the time). Listening is always a good idea in people work, but it is particularly important in giving feedback.

- *Keep a written record* People can resent being given feedback if they perceive it as criticism (even if you have bent over backwards to make it constructive and supportive) and may make a complaint. Having a record of what was said is therefore an important self-protection measure. It is, of course, also good practice to have a written record of important work you do.

- *Above all, be constructive* If you are giving negative feedback, it pays to help to develop ways forward, so that even criticism can be helpful if it is geared towards improvement and problem solving. If you are giving positive feedback, you can also look at how the situation can get even better.

A common approach to giving feedback that can be very helpful is what is known as the 'sandwich approach'. This involves beginning with positive feedback: 'I can see that you have made a lot of progress here in a number of areas', followed by any negative feedback that is needed: 'But, I do feel we need to look at those areas where progress has not been so good and consider why that might be', and finishing with positive feedback again: 'So, it is good to see that we have been able to identify areas of progress where you have done well and we've explored ways of sorting out those areas where progress is slow. I think this has been very constructive and I hope you agree.'

The dangers to avoid are the two unhelpful extremes of avoiding or fudging the issue on the one hand, and taking too hard a line on the other – see Figure 2.4. The healthy balance in between these two destructive extremes is a balanced, constructive approach based on principles of assertiveness (producing 'win–win' outcomes). In transactional analysis terms (see below), it is based on adult–adult interactions rather than parent–child.

Giving feedback does not have to be a difficult or anxiety-provoking activity. In fact, it can be an enjoyable and rewarding part of our work once we build up the confidence and skills to rise to the challenges involved.

| Not giving feedback or giving unclear feedback | Giving helpful feedback | Giving heavy-handed feedback |

Figure 2.4 Giving feedback

Helicopter vision
Obtaining an overview

The advantage of having access to a helicopter is that you can rise above a situation, get an overview, or 'the big picture', as it is often called, and then you can descend to the appropriate place where you can be of most help, where your intervention can have greatest impact. If you do not get this overview to begin with, then there is a danger that you will not know where and when to intervene. You may be drawn into intervening where the pressures or demands are greatest, but this will not necessarily be the place to achieve the greatest change or the best progress. Before tackling one part of a problem situation, it is wise to have at least some idea of how the different parts of that situation connect together and form the whole.

Sometimes we have to intervene rapidly in a situation where there is some sort of emergency, where there is risk to life and limb, for example. In such cases we may not have the relative luxury of being able to form an overview. We may have to respond there and then. However, in the grand scheme of things, such situations are relatively rare. The vast majority of situations where we are involved in trying to help people deal with their problems do give us at least some opportunity to get the feel of the situation and develop some sense of overview.

If we do not take advantage of the benefits of helicopter vision, we run the risk of allowing our intervention to rely too much on random factors. For example, we may choose to focus on a particular area because, from our particular standpoint, that seems to make sense. But from a different standpoint – the other side of the fence as it were – the situation may look very different. Helicopter vision would allow us to see both sides of the fence and the surrounding environment before deciding on the most appropriate place to focus our actions to try and be of help.

Helicopter vision can be of value at any stage in our intervention. It can be useful at the beginning to get an initial overview. It can be equally useful further down the line, once we have become involved in the situation we are trying to influence, to see whether our involvement has made any difference. This particular use of helicopter vision can be very beneficial, because sometimes we are focusing so much on our own part of the proceedings, as it were, that we do not realize what impact this may have made elsewhere in the situation – how, for example, our intervention may have had a domino effect, changing other aspects of the situation, perhaps without our immediate knowledge of it.

It can also be used when we are considering ending our involvement, as a sort of checking mechanism to see whether we feel it is safe to bring our involvement to a close or whether there are other things that need our attention before we can finally withdraw. Similarly, it can also be used when our intervention has finished, in order to evaluate our input to see what has worked (and whether it could have worked better), what did not work (how we could have done it differently) and what we have learned from the experience for future reference.

The technique of helicopter vision can be used as a guide to our own actions as described above. However, it can also be used as a tool of intervention in helping others. If the people we are trying to help have a tendency to focus narrowly on one aspect of their situation and not see how this relates to the bigger picture, then helping them to develop the skills of adopting helicopter vision can be a very beneficial way forward. For example, somebody who is depressed or anxious may see only the negative, worrying aspects of a situation and may need to be helped to develop a broader picture (see the discussion of 'SWOT analysis' below).

Helicopter vision also has application in working with groups or teams. It can be particularly helpful in situations characterized by conflict and disagreement. It can enable people to see how their perspective fits into the overall picture, thus highlighting where people are in agreement and where differences of perspective exist. This in itself will not resolve the difficulties, but it will provide a platform from which we can build on the areas of agreement and explore ways of dealing with the areas of conflict.

Mind maps (to be discussed below) can be used as one means of achieving helicopter vision, but it is not the only one. One very simple way to achieve helicopter vision is as follows:

- List the key people involved in the situation (those people who are significant in the development of the problem and possible solutions to it).
- Consider the situation from each person's point of view in turn.

- Next, consider the wider contextual factors. Is there anything significant about the context? Any power struggles, for example? Or hidden agendas?
- Finally, can you identify any common themes or linking threads? Anything that pulls the situation together and helps you make sense of it?

Do not worry if you find this process difficult at first. It can take some time to build up the skills of thinking holistically, which is, after all, what helicopter vision is all about.

Know your enemy
Coping with anxiety

Something that is very commonly encountered in people work is anxiety. This can apply in a number of ways. We can feel anxious ourselves in facing the challenges of helping people solve their problems. In many circumstances, anxiety will be a major part of the cause of the problems experienced by the people we are seeking to help, and even when anxiety is not in itself a cause or factor, it will often be present as a result of the problems – often exacerbating them. Anxiety can also exist at a wider level – for example, anxiety (and thus defensiveness) can be part of an organizational culture and can thus have a very significant impact on the work undertaken in that organization. For example, you may have a team of staff who are very limited and unadventurous in their approach because they have become 'risk averse', as a result of a defensive culture built on a degree of anxiety.

A major problem with anxiety is that it can become self-perpetuating. This is because a common response to anxiety is avoidance. That is, if something is making us anxious, we are likely to seek to avoid it. While that is a perfectly understandable reaction, it is not always a helpful one. 'Avoidance behaviour', as psychologists call it, can be a significant barrier to progress. What it refers to is the tendency for people to, in effect, run away from their problems rather than face up to them and try and deal with them. There are two major problems with this. First, it can lead to a vicious circle. That is, the more we avoid our problems, the more anxious we can become in certain circumstances at least, and thus the more anxious we become, the more we avoid our problems, and so it goes on. Second, avoidance behaviour can lead to other problems. For example, if I am anxious about dealing with person X and therefore avoid doing so, I may subsequently face the situation of having a complaint made against me by person X because of my failure to undertake my duties in respect of him or her (see the discussion of 'Avoiding avoidance' above).

Another significant aspect of anxiety and avoidance behaviour is that the situation can change without our recognizing it, thus leaving us in a position of avoidance when in fact there is nothing left to avoid. For example, consider a situation where I avoid dealing with an aggressive man because his aggressive behaviour makes me anxious. It may well be the case that this man was being aggressive because of something that was bothering him. However, the situation may have now changed whereby he is no longer feeling distressed and is no longer responding in an aggressive way. However, if my tactic for dealing with the anxiety he generated in me was to avoid him, then I may well continue avoiding him for some considerable time after he has ceased to be aggressive.

One very useful way of dealing with anxiety is to translate it into fear. This is because anxiety tends to be generalized (when we are anxious we tend to have an overall feeling of uneasiness), whereas fear tends to be specific – fear *of* something. By making our generalized feeling of anxiety more specific, we can get a better picture of what is bothering us and what we need to do to deal with it. In this way, we are able to 'know our enemy', to be clear about precisely what is causing us problems. We are then much better equipped to deal with whatever it is that is causing concern. The following dialogue should help to illustrate this:

Anwen: You seem to be very anxious. What's troubling you?
Pat: I don't know, I just feel very uneasy about the way things are at the moment.
Anwen: Is there anything in particular that you can put your finger on?
Pat: Well, I hadn't really thought about it until now, but I suppose I'm mainly worried about all the uncertainty that's around.
Anwen: Yes, uncertainty can be very unsettling. But is there anything in particular that you dread? Anything that you are afraid might happen?

Pat: Erm ... well, I suppose it all comes down to wondering whether I will be able to cope with it all.

Anwen: You're frightened it will be too much for you?

Pat: Yes.

Anwen: In what way?

Pat: There's an awful lot expected of me just now, and I'm not sure I've got what it takes to come up with the goods. I suppose I'm having a crisis of confidence.

Anwen: You're frightened that you will be seen to fail?

Pat: Yes, exactly. Yes, you've hit the nail on the head.

Anwen: So, would it help for us to look at what exactly is being expected of you and how you might cope with that?

Pat: Yes, I think it would. Thank you, I've started to feel better about it already.

Anwen: That's good. I think it's always better to be clear about what's worrying us, rather than let general feelings of anxiety undermine us.

This provides a clear example of how 'knowing your enemy' puts you at an advantage compared with the generally unsettling feeling of anxiety. Sometimes helping people realize precisely what is bothering them is all that they need – they can now tackle those issues themselves once they have had your help in pinpointing them. However, in other situations, identifying what the fears are is only the beginning of a longer, more detailed piece of work in terms of working out how best to deal with them. None the less, in either case, the use of this technique will have taken us a significant step forward.

The example given in the dialogue above is on a one-to-one basis. However, the same technique can also be used with groups of people (families or teams, for example) and, of course, we can also use it to help ourselves when we are feeling anxious – helping people deal with problems does not make us immune from them ourselves!

Making the most of meetings
Avoiding time and energy being wasted

Meetings can be vitally important events that play a key role in solving problems, securing progress and pulling people together towards a common goal. Unfortunately, though, they can also be a complete waste of time. Poor meetings can be very wasteful because:

- the time costs are multiplied (ten people attending a two-hour meeting that produces no benefits means that a total of 20 hours has been wasted – almost the equivalent of three full days);
- the time involved in the meeting itself is not all that is wasted – there will be arrangement time (getting the meeting set up), preparation time (participants reading documents and so on) and travelling time (the total time wasted for an unproductive meeting could therefore actually add up to the equivalent of a full week of an individual's time);
- in addition to the time costs, there will be financial costs in terms of heating, lighting, travel expenses plus possibly venue hire and refreshment costs;
- the opportunity costs are significant – not only is time wasted, but opportunities to make significant progress can also be lost;
- they can create a lot of bad feeling and demotivate people, thus contributing further to waste of time as demotivated people will be less productive.

An unproductive meeting can therefore be very wasteful indeed. Meetings can be unproductive for a number of reasons, not least the following:

- *The wrong people are present*   Sometimes people who do not need to be at a meeting are invited, perhaps because the person doing the inviting did not think the issues through well enough (or was ill-informed about the purpose or focus of the meeting) or perhaps because some people attend certain meetings out of habit or a misplaced sense of duty, even when they have little to contribute to or gain from that particular meeting.
- *The right people are absent*   That is, people who should have been there are not. If a certain person's input to a meeting is crucial, but he or she cannot be there, a lot of time can be wasted.

- *The timing is wrong* This can apply in two senses. First, it can relate to situations where it would have been better to discuss the subject matter of the meeting after a related decision has been made (the meeting is premature) or to situations where events have already overtaken the agenda (the meeting is too late). Second, it can relate to poorly scheduled meetings – for example, a meeting to discuss complex matters late on a Friday afternoon when most people are least well equipped to handle complex issues.
- *The meeting is badly chaired* An inexperienced, unskilled or biased chair can wreak havoc with a meeting, perhaps wasting everyone's time and lowering morale and motivation. However (and this is a point I shall return to below), what can make matters worse is when participants collude with poor chairing and basically let him or her get away with it.
- *Minutes are unhelpful, non-existent or too late* Sometimes minutes are expressed in such a cryptic way that even people who were present at the meeting do not know what they refer to. Sometimes minutes disappear or none were taken in the first place. At other times, they may be produced only on the day of the next meeting (or shortly beforehand), which means that people who agreed to undertake particular tasks at the last meeting have not received a timely reminder.
- *The meeting is overloaded* It is not unusual for meetings to have long and unrealistic agendas. This can mean that people are trying to achieve too much in the time available, resulting in some issues being glossed over or not being discussed at all. Overloaded meetings can also fail because the competition for particular items to receive attention can lead to all sorts of (potentially destructive) political games being played.
- *Hidden agendas dominate* Sometimes the formal agenda bears little resemblance to the actual issues that are at stake. Again this can mean potentially destructive political games being played.

Clearly, then, there are many ways in which meetings can go awry. When we balance this against how important meetings can be in determining the outcomes of problem situations (in terms of decision making, gaining access to resources and so on), we can see just how important it is to make sure that meetings are not allowed to fail. If we fall into the trap of allowing meetings to be a waste of time, effort and resources, then we will be undermining our own effectiveness as problem solvers. How, then, can we make sure that we make the most of meetings? The following guidelines are not exhaustive but should give you some pointers for trying to make meetings you are involved with a success:

1. *Do your homework* Is there any preparation you need to do before the meeting to make sure you get the most out of it?

2. *Focus on purpose* What do you want the meeting to achieve for you (and thus for the person(s) you are trying to help)? Keep a clear focus on this.

3. *Don't collude with poor chairing* If the meeting has drifted off the agenda or is spending more time on an item than it deserves, then it is the primary responsibility of the chair to rectify the situation. Note, however, that I say *primary,* rather than *sole* responsibility. Everyone in a meeting has a responsibility for making it a successful, effective gathering, not just the chair. However, it is very common for poor chairing to result in poor outcomes because other participants did not do their bit. For example, they did not say things like: 'I am concerned about Item 4 on the agenda and I am anxious that we might not have time to discuss it if we do not move on soon' or 'These are important issues that have come up, but they are not on the agenda for this meeting, so I propose we discuss them at another time and press on with our agenda'. If done tactfully and assertively, rather than aggressively, such comments can be very effective.

4. *Treat time with respect* There is no need to rush – indeed, too much haste can be highly problematic, but do be conscious of time constraints. If you have something to say, do not go all round the houses – state your point(s) clearly and effectively. Meetings are an exercise in communication, so use your communication skills to maximum advantage by getting your message across clearly and crisply without any need for embellishment or unnecessary detail. In particular, be wary of allowing any anxiety about speaking in public to lead you into waffling. It only serves to put you in the limelight for longer than is necessary and runs the risk of annoying your colleagues.

Mind mapping
Developing a picture of the situation you are dealing with

This is a technique associated with the work of Tony Buzan (Buzan and Buzan, 2003). A mind map is a visual representation of a set of ideas or issues and how they interrelate. Preparing a mind map can be very useful, partly because it provides a helpful overview of the range of issues you are dealing with and how they are connected, and partly because the process itself can be useful in its own right – it can help to give a sense of control and confidence in dealing with a set of difficult issues.

Mind maps can be used in various ways. They can be used to clarify your own thinking, to help other people clarify their thinking, or as a group exercise. I have found them particularly useful when people are under stress because they have too many plates spinning – that is, they feel that their life is overcomplicated. Producing a mind map can give an overview of the situation and show how the different elements interrelate. That in itself can be a useful form of intervention.

To draw a mind map you will need a sheet of A4 paper or similar. First, turn it on its side so that it is 'landscape' layout. At the centre of the page write the focus of the map – for example, if your focus for this particular mind map is a current project you are involved with, then write the name of the project at the centre. Alternatively, you may wish to come up with some sort of drawing or visual symbol to represent the project. From this central point, you will need to draw thick lines outwards, one each for the various themes that characterize the project. For example, if one set of projects is around reviewing activities, then write 'reviewing activities' along that particular line. These themes emerging from the central point should be written in capital letters. The lines should be roughly the same length as the words written on them, although this is not crucial.

Once you have identified these main themes, go through each of them systematically and, for each of them, draw lines outwards from the end of the thick line and, on each of these lines, write the particular issues or projects. Continue this process with each of the themes until you have an overview of the situation you are now addressing. What you should end up with is something like Figure 2.5, with a central core concept from which the main themes radiate, each with its sub-themes branching out.

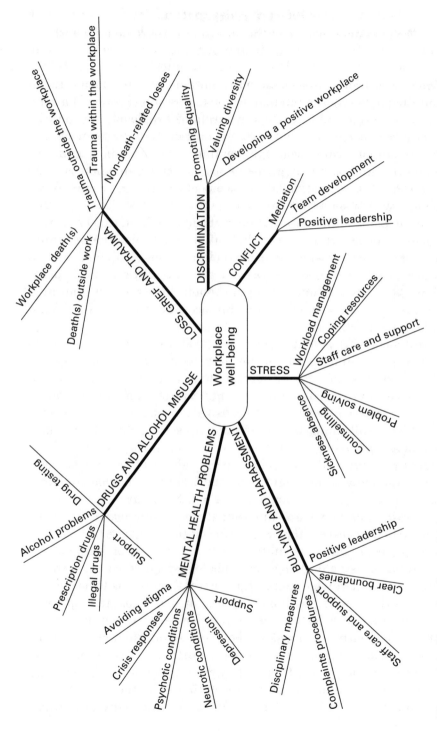

Figure 2.5 Example of a mind map

Mind mapping is based on the idea that the brain does not think in straight lines, that our thinking, in other words, is not linear. We tend to jump from one issue to another, but this tends to be not in a random way but, rather, across a connection of interlocking themes and issues. The mind map is intended to be a visual representation of that set of interconnected themes and issues. This non-linear representation can be very useful for at least two reasons. First, it enables us to jump from one part of the map to another as we see fit. This can encourage creativity and a more imaginative approach. Second, it can enable us to see connections that we may perhaps not have previously noticed. For example, I once did a mind map with somebody who was depressed. It was only through producing this mind map that he realized how frequently financial matters cropped up in it. This helped him to realize that a significant part of his problem was financial worries. However, he had been so depressed that he was not thinking clearly and had not been able to work this out, even though, once we saw the mind map, it was perfectly clear that finances were a very significant part of his worries.

Mind maps are generally seen as a good way of helping people to develop their thinking skills. However, in my experience, they also have implications in terms of the other two aspects of 'Think–feel–do' (discussed below), namely emotions and actions. I have experience of using mind maps with people who are anxious, with the result being that they become less anxious. I also have experience of using mind maps with people who were perhaps being overconfident (see the discussion above of 'Doing the right things vs. doing things right') and the technique has been helpful in enabling them to develop a more realistic picture – for example, by showing just how many different strands there may be involved in a particular project they are planning to undertake.

Some people like to be quite artistic in their use of mind maps – for example, using drawings or symbols instead of words. If this is something that you feel comfortable with, then this is to be encouraged, as the idea of the mind map is that it is a tool to help you – it is not a set of rules to restrict you. However, if you do not feel comfortable with drawings, symbols and so on, then by all means stick to words. This will not cause any problems. It is simply a case of finding the approach that suits you or, if you are helping other people to do mind maps, the approach that suits them.

Mind maps can be very powerful tools, and many people use

them extensively. If you feel that mind mapping is something that appeals to you and that you are likely to draw upon in your future work, then you are strongly encouraged to read the *Mind Map Book* (Buzan and Buzan, 2003), as this book provides detailed but relatively simple guidance on how to develop your skills in mind mapping. It also provides lots of useful examples of mind maps that can help to give you a clearer picture of what is involved and how it can be used.

Modelling and use of self
Using yourself as a tool to help others

The idea of apprenticeship has a long history, especially in trade and craft occupations. Much of the learning involved in apprenticeship is based on the idea of the apprentice watching the 'master' in action and, to a certain extent, copying what he or she is doing. In the people professions, simply copying what somebody else does can be dangerous. This is because the particular style adopted by that person may be something that is based on years of experience and the knowledge and skills that have developed during that time. Someone without that knowledge and those skills could get into serious difficulties by simply copying what a more experienced worker does.

However, this is not to say that there is no room at all for a modelling approach. There is indeed much to be gained by watching a skilful people worker in action. The point is that we must then take that basic learning and adapt it to suit our own circumstances, our own strengths and our own areas for development. Simply copying is not enough.

Modelling as a tool can be very helpful in helping others to sort their problems out. For example, where somebody is experiencing difficulty in managing a range of pressures they face, it can be helpful for someone to sit down with them and help them set priorities. What is important to note, however, is that issues of modelling should not be allowed to become simply doing something *for* someone. Helping somebody to set their priorities is not the same as setting their priorities for them. However, by going through the process together, a skilled worker can not only achieve the desired result, but also teach the individual concerned some skills so that he or she will be in a stronger position to achieve that result on their own next time.

There is quite an art in doing things *with* people rather than *for* them, but it is an important art to develop. This is because doing something for someone may actually hinder their development. You may make them more dependent and less self-sufficient, and therefore in a weaker position to deal with their problems, rather than in a stronger one.

Modelling can also be used in team or group settings. For example, if you have a group member who is especially good at a particular skill, then he or she can be asked to demonstrate that skill to others, so that they have the opportunity to learn from it. This can have the added bonus of encouraging teamwork, as it discourages a competitive approach and supports the idea of people learning from one another. Group members can see others within the group as collaborators rather than competitors.

Linked to modelling is the idea of 'use of self'. In modelling, we are using our own skills and experience to help others. Use of self means going beyond this to help people learn from our knowledge and skills and experience in other ways. A simple example of this would be: in a situation where someone is feeling guilty and disheartened because they have failed at a particular task, it may be helpful for the helper to explain that he or she also failed at that task at some time in the past but learned from the experience and none the less made progress. This approach can be very helpful, but there are two caveats. First, it is important not to overdo this – for example, by revealing too much personal detail about oneself, as this can undermine our professional credibility.

Second, it is important to be genuine in use of self. I have come across examples of people who have made up stories in order to mimic the use of self. For example, to return to my earlier example, someone may claim to have failed at the same thing without actually having done so. This is a very risky strategy because, if it subsequently emerges that this was a lie, any trust developed with that person could be easily destroyed and the chances of rebuilding such trust would be minimal indeed. There are also, of course, ethical issues about lying to somebody you are trying to help.

To help you in the development of use of self, it can be beneficial for you to think of the different areas you are likely to be dealing with in your work as a people problem solver, perhaps listing these on a sheet of paper or drawing a mind map. Once you have done this, you can then look back over your life experience and think of situations where you faced problems similar, in some respect at least, to the ones that you are likely to be called upon to deal with. For example, if your work is likely to bring you into contact with people who are experiencing a lot of anxiety, what anxious situations have you encountered in your life? How did you deal with them? How did you manage to conquer them and move forward?

Of course, it is important to realize that this is not simply a matter of advising people to follow your lead, to take the steps that you took (or to avoid the mistakes that you made), as it is unlikely that the parallels between their situation and yours will be quite that simple. However, with careful consideration, you should be able to find at least some links between your experience and theirs. This can also have the added benefit of increasing trust and providing a solid foundation for a positive working relationship.

In using the technique of use of self, be careful not to go to extremes. If you give many examples of mistakes you have made, you may come across as somebody who is constantly making mistakes and this could undermine your credibility in the eyes of the people you are working with. At the other extreme, if you are constantly giving examples of how you have managed to do well in certain situations, then you may come across as arrogant and unconnected with the reality of the problems being faced. These are both clearly situations to avoid.

Modelling and use of self both indicate that, while each person's circumstances and challenges will be unique in some ways, there are also likely to be common dimensions. There are likely to be places within the problem situation where that individual's experience can connect with other people's experience, thus giving them some degree of a sense of sharing and common endeavour. In trying to help somebody resolve their difficulties, this can be a very valuable asset.

Naming the process
Bringing hidden agendas out into the open

Sometimes there are destructive or harmful processes going on in interactions between people, but they are going on at a submerged level – that is, they are happening 'beneath the table' rather than 'on the table', as it were, like a hidden agenda at a meeting. Sometimes the use of such processes is deliberate – for example, when somebody is trying to sabotage a particular event or process because it is not in their interests for it to succeed. Very often, though, the underlying harmful process is not deliberate, it is the historical result of various factors that have come together to produce this outcome. For example, the fears of various individuals may combine to produce a situation in which particular topics become taboo because no one feels comfortable in raising or tackling them. This is not necessarily a deliberate plan, but arises through very complex and subtle processes of interaction between individuals and across groups. We shall first of all consider how naming the process can be used to deal with the deliberate use of destructive processes by one or more people and then move on to consider how the technique can be used to counter less deliberate but what can be equally damaging processes.

An example of a deliberate, underlying, harmful process would be where somebody chooses to avoid a particular topic by changing the subject whenever this topic arises. It is in circumstances like these that the technique of naming the process can be very useful. For example, if you become aware that somebody is changing the subject whenever you raise an important issue, you may make this visible by 'naming the process' – that is, you may expressly say 'I've noticed that whenever I raise the matter of x, you change the subject. Why is that?' You may then want to follow this up with a comment such as: 'Is there a problem there I can help you with?' (see also the discussion above of 'Avoiding avoidance').

An example of a less deliberate use of destructive processes would be a situation known as 'groupthink'. This is a term used by Janis (1982) to refer to the tendency for groups of people (including teams) to fail to challenge assumptions about the group and what it is doing – the desire not to spoil a nice team atmosphere, for example, can mean that important but potentially conflictual issues are not raised. Practice focus 2.5 shows how this can work.

Other examples of how harmful processes can arise without any deliberate intention can be found in relation to various forms of discrimination. For example, institutional racism refers to forms of racial discrimination that are not direct and deliberate (personal racism), but rather which have arisen over time due to discriminatory practices or assumptions that have become part of working practices and organizational culture. Indeed, this is what makes institutional racism difficult to eradicate – it is not simply a matter of disciplining an individual perpetrator, it is a much more difficult job of changing institutionalized practices.

Although institutionalized racism has received a great deal of media attention, it is not the only form of institutionalized discrimination. For example, institutionalized sexism is also very prevalent – where women are treated in a patronizing way, not as part of a deliberate attempt to cause offence, but out of a naïve lack of awareness of gender equality issues. Older and/or disabled people also face such problems. Naming the process can play an important role in tackling such issues.

In using this technique, it is very important to recognize just how powerful it is. If we are to use the analogy of tools (comparing the techniques in this book with tools used in a physical sense), then naming the process is the equivalent of a chainsaw – that is, it is extremely powerful and therefore very dangerous if used inappropriately. It should not be used lightly. It is best used in circumstances where:

1. you have a good working relationship with the person concerned;
2. the situation is sufficiently important to warrant taking the risk;
3. you feel sufficiently confident in the circumstances that you can deal with the reaction to your use of the tool.

Of course, in using any tool or technique, there is always a risk that the situation will backfire but in using this particularly powerful technique, the risk is greater and the harm that can be done is also greater. It should therefore be used with great caution. Just imagine, for example, how you might react if somebody used this technique with you.

None the less, despite these notes of caution, this is a very helpful tool when used appropriately and can make for a situation where great progress is achieved in a short period of time. It can cut through issues that could otherwise stand in the way of progress.

Over the years the company Tom worked for had developed a very distinctive way of working. They had their own way of dealing with the various tasks they undertook. They were proud of doing everything 'their way'. However, when Tom started attending his part-time Diploma course, he began to realize that there were other ways of doing things. He became aware that there were ways in which things could be improved at work. However, when he raised this with his colleagues, they basically ignored him. He tried time and time again and got nowhere, becoming more and more frustrated as time went by. In the end he decided to raise this in supervision. He again met resistance and, feeling even more frustrated, asked directly: 'Why does this company seem to have such a closed mind when it comes to looking at new ideas? Every time I suggest something new, it gets pushed aside.' His supervisor was a bit taken a back by this, but it did open the door for discussing the company's attitude to outside influences and whether or not there was a problem in this respect. Tom was delighted that he was starting to get somewhere at last.

Not tolerating vagueness
Avoiding the dangers of being too vague

In some circumstances, it is essential to be very precise indeed. For example, in some engineering situations it is necessary to provide measurements within very fine fractions of whatever unit is being measured. Life in general, however, does not normally require that degree of precision, and it is perhaps inevitable that a degree of vagueness creeps in. However, when we are working with people and their problems, it can sometimes be disastrous to allow vagueness to become a feature of our work. In my view, an important principle of problem solving is to be clear about precisely what we are dealing with. Any indecision can lead to our heading off in the wrong direction or adopting the wrong approach. Consider, for example, the discussion of systematic practice in Part One of this book. If we were to be vague about what we are trying to achieve, how we are going to achieve it or how we will know when we have achieved it, then the whole process could be undermined. This does not mean that we have to be precise to a scientific degree on all occasions, but it does mean that there is a danger in allowing vagueness to undermine what we are doing.

Practice focus 2.6 below illustrates clearly how we can create problems rather than solve them by being vague. As I have argued previously, the people we are trying to help:

> are often in a state of confusion by virtue of the particular problems they face. If we are not careful, we can add to this state of confusion by being vague and unfocused. In situations characterized by confusion and a lack of direction, the people worker's role is often that of an 'anchor', providing a degree of stability, security and clarity. An unfocused approach can therefore not only fail to fulfil this important role, but also add to the confusion and instability. (2002a, p. 174)

Note, however, that the title of this particular tool is not simply 'Not being vague', but rather 'Not tolerating vagueness'. This adds an extra dimension. While we may put a lot of effort into ensuring our own actions and communications are not plagued with vagueness, in addition we need to go a step further in trying to make sure that those communications we receive, and the actions of other people, are also not plagued with vagueness. This means that we need to have fairly well-developed interpersonal skills to be able to challenge vagueness in a constructive way that will not alienate others. If we simply say to somebody, 'That's very vague, please be more precise', this can easily be interpreted as a direct criticism and can result in unnecessary tensions and obstacles to making progress. We therefore have to become very skilled in asking the appropriate questions in the appropriate ways.

Sometimes people will be deliberately vague – that is, they will be doing this because they have something to hide or there is something they feel uncomfortable discussing. However, it is often the case that people are being vague because they have not thought through the issues, or it is a characteristic mode of communication. It is therefore important not to assume that someone who is being vague is definitely concealing something deliberately. That is quite a big assumption to make and sometimes a dangerous one.

However, where there are grounds to suspect that somebody is being deliberately vague, we have to handle the situation very carefully. A useful principle to adopt here is that of finding the balance between, on the one hand, simply allowing them to continue to be vague and, on the other, pushing them so hard that we risk 'getting their back up'.

Dealing with somebody in such circumstances can easily lead us into a situation that is quite characteristic of this notion of not tolerating vagueness – namely the situation where we have to be gently persistent by continuing to pursue the issue. For example, someone may be quite vague in response to a question, and so our next question pursues the matter further, at which point the person concerned may reveal a little more information, but not much. We will therefore need to probe a little further and continue probing until it becomes clear to the person we are dealing with that we are maintaining that constructive balance between simply letting it go and alienating him or her. This has much in common with the notion of 'assertiveness'. Basically, what it involves is trying to find a win–win solution; a situation where the person you are communicating with does not feel harassed, but where you are not left feeling that you have failed to get the important information that you need to help him or her.

Not tolerating vagueness is not a technique to be used at specific times but, rather, a general tool to be used whenever we are dealing with other people. There may well be particular times (for example, when somebody is being deliberately vague) where we need to use our skills in this area to the full, but my argument would be that we need to be practising these skills at all times. In any interaction with other people there is the danger that we will allow vagueness to creep in, and thus cause problems in our attempts to resolve the difficulties being experienced. Vagueness, then, is clearly an enemy of effective problem solving and we should do everything we reasonably can to make sure that it is not allowed to sabotage the work we undertake.

Practice focus 2.6

Jan told her line manager that she was concerned about Peter because he could be demanding and this made her feel uncomfortable. Her line manager told her this was part of the job and only to be expected. He told her she would have to get used to it. The next day Jan went to visit Peter to discuss his plans. He became more and more agitated until he became so worked up that he assaulted her.

When Jan's line manager found out what had happened, he was very supportive. He asked her if she had had any indication Peter might become violent, to which she replied that she had already told him that she was concerned about Peter. 'Yes, but you didn't mention any threat of violence, did you?' to which she replied: 'I told you I wasn't happy working with him and you said I had to get used to it'.

Jan had been vague in expressing her concerns to her line manager and had not spelled out her concerns about the risk of violence and her line manager had not pressed her to be more precise about what she meant by 'demanding' and 'uncomfortable' – he had tolerated her vagueness and thus missed an important opportunity to help her, and save her from harm.

Objectives tree
A framework for helping to develop plans

In Part One of the book, the importance of keeping a clear focus on what we are trying to achieve was emphasized. One way of doing this is to make use of what is known as an objectives tree. This involves drawing a diagram. Figure 2.6 provides a worked example of this.

At the top of the page we put a box in which we write our over-all aim – that is the particular outcome that we are seeking to bring about. From this box we have lines connecting to other boxes which contain the main elements that will contribute to the achievement of the objective in the top box. For example, if our desired outcome is better communication, then in the boxes on the second tier of the objectives tree we would have those elements that contribute to better communication (clear systems, well-chaired meetings, a culture based on collaboration and so on).

There is no rule about how many boxes there should be. This will vary from situation to situation and group to group. It could be anything between two and twelve or perhaps even more in some circumstances. We should be careful not to rush into deciding what these second-tier 'boxes' should be. The tool should be used to encourage careful reflection on what it is we are trying to achieve (the overall aim in the first-tier box).

From each of these second-tier boxes we then need to draw out a list of the actions that need to be taken to bring about what is written in the particular box. When we have completed this list for each of the second-tier boxes, we will then have in effect a road map from bottom to top. That is, if we look at the steps to be taken that have been identified deriving from each of the second-tier boxes, these should then lead us to success in terms of achieving the desired outcome at second level which, in turn, will contribute

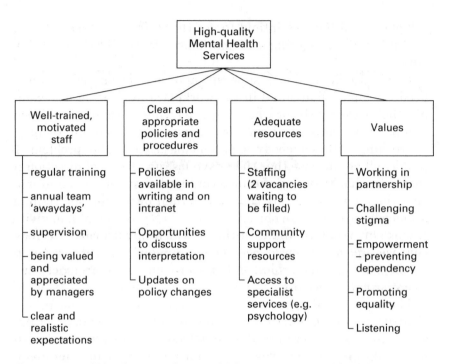

Figure 2.6 Objectives tree for a multidisciplinary mental health team

to achieving to the overall aim in the main box at the top of the page.

This is a very simple form of objectives tree and, to begin with, it helps to keep it simple until you are familiar with the technique. However, it can also be used in a more advanced form so that, for example, we can have third-tier boxes that feed into the second-tier boxes and from each of the three-tier boxes, we then have a list of steps that need to be taken. Such steps can then be broken down into further sub-steps. The whole objectives tree can then become very complex (in the same way as a mind map can – see the discussion of 'Mind mapping' above). Some people choose to use a white board, for example, to draw such a complex and large objectives tree. Using a white board or equivalent also gives the flexibility of being able to amend the diagram without having to start from scratch with a fresh piece of paper.

This technique can be used at a number of different levels. It can be used by an individual worker or manager as a tool for focusing one's thinking. It can help to clarify in our own mind where we are going and how we intend to get there. In this respect, it is a useful tool for promoting systematic practice as discussed in Part One.

It can also be used as a supervision or mentoring tool. It can be used to help an individual in the workplace to focus on, for example, their career goals or what they are trying to achieve in relation to a particular project. It can also be used as a tool of intervention in working with somebody experiencing a particular problem. It could well be the case that they have lost any sense of direction in their life, that they have become confused, disorientated and may be acting in ways that are contrary to their own interests. Helping somebody to develop an objectives tree can be very helpful in giving a sense of structure and direction – which in turn can give reassurance and boost confidence. This can be of particular value to people experiencing either confusion or depression or anxiety or a combination of the three.

The tool can also be used as a team development technique. That is, on a team-building day, a staff team can be divided into sub-groups, each given a sheet of flipchart paper and asked to undertake the task of developing an objectives tree for the team. This can be followed by a feedback session where the team members look at each other's objectives tree diagrams on the flipcharts displayed on the wall and then have what can be a fruitful discussion about similarities and differences. Ideally, this could lead them to developing a unified objectives tree based on the combination of factors arising from the separate objectives trees produced by the sub-groups. I have undertaken this exercise myself with a number of teams and it has proven very valuable in identifying:

1.   common ground and consensus that can be built on; and
2.   areas of conflict that need further exploration and resolution.

This is a technique that you may find difficult at first. However, I would recommend that you practise using it, and it is then likely that you will become increasingly skilled and confident over time. The more confident and skilful you are in using the technique, the more confidence others will have in you when you help them to develop their own objectives trees.

Paint the toilets
Making a fresh start

Some problems emerge very quickly in a short period of time. However, very many more problems are the result of perhaps years of slow and steady development (or deterioration). The problem situation you are asked to deal with today may have begun to develop many years ago. Often we are dealing with entrenched problems, issues that have perhaps become part of the culture of an organization or group of people. Problems can have long histories and deep roots. In such circumstances, developing solutions can take a great deal of time – implementing those solutions perhaps even longer. A set of problems that have developed over a period of years may equally take years to resolve.

While patience is clearly a virtue, it is not always present in great abundance in circumstances where people have been encountering problems for a considerable time, where their frustration level is high and their tolerance level is low. When you are faced with the challenge of trying to resolve deeply ingrained long-term problems, you may find that patience runs very thin for some people and that you are facing considerable pressure to produce significant results in a short period of time. Often these expectations will be unrealistic and unreasonable but borne of the frustration experienced by the people concerned over an extended period of time. It is important to resist the temptation to promise to meet such unrealistic demands, but it is important, in order to ensure that the situation does not boil over and that you do not lose the good will and co-operation of the people concerned, that you make a quick and notable contribution to alleviating the situation. This is referred to as the 'paint the toilets', technique because sometimes it can be literally by making such a small but significant and noticeable change that a clear message is put forward – namely that change has begun, that the 'beginning of the end' of the problems has been reached. In an organization it gives a clear message of 'Under new management'. Of course, this is not enough in itself, but it can be a very useful start to make a small but significant change.

The technique involves identifying a small change that can have a big impact, something that can be done quickly and effectively, but which could have a significant result in terms of giving a very clear message – we are taking this situation seriously and we are doing our best to put it right. The goodwill that can be generated by this can buy you time and help to generate an atmosphere where patience is more likely to be the order of the day, rather than frustration and a sense that nothing is happening.

In using this technique, it is vitally important not to allow it to become seen as tokenistic. If you literally or metaphorically paint the toilets and then do nothing further, then the whole process can prove counterproductive. It can mean that any negativity that has developed over the years will be reinforced rather than broken down. It is therefore important that you make sure that the 'paint the toilets' technique is used appropriately – namely as a technique for making a short-term, significant impact to buy a little bit of time and patience to make the other changes that are necessary. It is, of course, not an alternative to making those changes. In fact, it can be very counterproductive to get off to a good start and then not follow this up. You can easily end up in a worse situation than where you started.

The tool can be used in working with individuals – where we could perhaps identify something that would ease their problems, that could be implemented relatively swiftly and effectively (without causing other problems) and make this happen. In this way we can help to establish a relationship of trust and, where necessary, challenge any feelings of helplessness and hopelessness (such feelings are not uncommon where people have been experiencing apparently insoluble problems over a period of time).

The tool can also be used in working with families, groups or teams on pretty much the same basis – that is, finding something that can make a positive difference very quickly, with a view to creating a positive impact, trying to generate a sense of hope.

Of course, there is no guarantee that this technique will work. Some people will be so immersed in a sense of defeatism that they will not be impressed by even a very positive change. However, even in these circumstances, the tool is likely to be worth using because such attitudes may take a long time to change, but at least you have made a step in the right direction – and that can be very important in laying the foundations for progress at a later date. In dealing with families, groups or teams, you may encounter a mixed response. That is, some people may respond positively while others remain cynical. Where this occurs it gives you the opportunity to try and build on the positives and try and tilt the balance in that direction.

PCS analysis
Understanding different levels of discrimination

This is a framework that I have discussed at length in my other work (Thompson, 1995; 2003a; 2006) specifically in relation to issues associated with discrimination. However, it can also be used more broadly as a means of understanding the important interrelationships across different levels of analysis – the different levels or dimensions of human experience.

PCS analysis is based on the idea that there are three interconnected levels that need to be taken into consideration if we are to develop an adequate understanding of discrimination in particular and human experience in general. PCS is shorthand for personal, cultural and structural:

- *Personal* This refers to the level of the individual and reminds us that we must not lose sight of the perspective, interests and needs of the individuals we are seeking to help. People's behaviour will, of course, depend largely on how they perceive the world, on what their experiences mean to them. In problem solving it is therefore a significant mistake to neglect the personal dimension.
- *Cultural* While the personal dimension is clearly important, we should not limit ourselves to considering matters from an individualistic point of view. Although each of us is indeed a unique individual, we are also part of wider cultural patterns and formations – we will have been brought up in a particular cultural context (and thus have been heavily influenced by it) and will now be operating currently within a cultural context. Our current cultural influences may complement or conflict with the cultural context of our upbringing, but either way it will be a significant influence on our behaviour and our understanding of the world. In trying to understand the people we are seeking to help, it would therefore be a major mistake to fail to take account of cultural issues – the shared meanings and 'unwritten rules' that play such an important role in shaping our experiences and thus our lives.
- *Structural* The society in which we live and work is not a level playing field. It is divided up into 'sub-groups' that form a structured network. Who we are, how we perceive the world

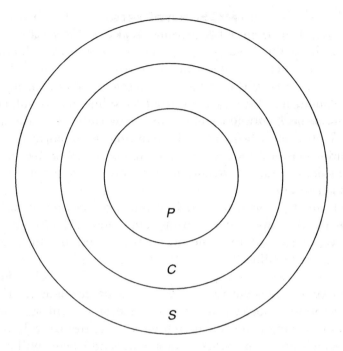

Figure 2.7   PCS analysis
Source: Thompson (2006).

and so on will depend upon not only our personal circumstances, not only on the cultural formations that we were
brought up in and now live in, but also on where we fit into
the structure of society based on class, gender, race and so on.
Power and opportunities in life are not distributed evenly
across society, and this uneven distribution will have a significant bearing on an individual's identity and broader social
circumstances. For example, it is clear that someone born into
poverty will have a very different upbringing from someone
born into great wealth.

The basis of PCS analysis is that, if we want to develop an
adequate understanding of the people we are trying to help, we
need to take account of all three dimensions: their *personal*
perspective and life experiences to date, the *cultural* influences
that continue to shape those life experiences (and our reactions to
them) and the *structural* context of an uneven distribution of power
and opportunities.

PCS analysis is a *dynamic* model – that is, it is based on an interaction of the three levels (a moving picture rather than a snapshot). An individual's sense of self (personal) will be influenced by culture and structure, but culture and structure are also influenced by the cumulative effect of individual actions over time. Similarly, cultural ideas influence and are influenced by structural factors.

This approach can be used in working with individuals, groups, families or even whole organizations or communities. It is an analytical tool for making sure that we do not adopt too narrow a focus on the individual without considering the wider cultural and structural context.

In terms of problem solving by promoting change, it has to be recognized that we have a decreasing level of influence from personal to cultural to structural levels. That is, influencing a culture is more difficult than influencing an individual, and influencing a structure is likely to be an even more difficult undertaking. We therefore have to be realistic in acknowledging that we may not be in a position to change cultural or structural factors (except on a long-term, collective basis); appreciating how these wider levels have an impact on the personal level will help us develop a fuller picture of the circumstances we are dealing with (see the discussion of sociopolitical challenges in Part One).

Practice focus 2.7

Jonathan enjoyed the course on equality and diversity and was particularly interested in the presentation about PCS analysis, as this gave him a much broader perspective than he had previously had. He started to consider his workload in terms of the three dimensions – personal, cultural and structural – instead of concentrating only on the individual level as he had done before. At first he felt a little daunted when he realized how complex situations became when viewed in terms of three dimensions instead of just one. However, once he realized how it deepened his understanding of the situations he faced, he recognized that it would be a useful tool for making sure he did not adopt too narrow a perspective.

By seeing many of the situations he encountered in his work as having three dimensions, rather than just one, he began to appreciate how, in the past, he had tended to oversimplify issues, especially those relating to discrimination. He had tended to see discrimination as primarily, if not solely, a matter of personal prejudice. Being introduced to PCS analysis had enabled him to develop a much more sophisticated understanding of these issues.

Positive strokes
Building confidence

When we are involved in helping people to sort out their problems, we face the risk of what is known as an occupational bias. That is, because we can so easily become engrossed in problems, we may have a tendency to concentrate primarily on problems and difficulties without necessarily balancing them out with positives (see the discussion of 'SWOT analysis' below). Being able to balance positives and negatives is a key skill for people problem solvers. However, because of the occupational bias we face, it is often necessary for us to make sure that we are accentuating the positives, that we are highlighting strengths and assets and valuing these as fully as we can. This can be particularly important when we are dealing with people whose confidence or self-esteem levels are low – a situation quite common when people are experiencing problems, as the problems themselves may be a source of low self-esteem (or may have been caused in part at least by pre-existing low self-esteem).

The idea behind positive strokes is that we should take every reasonable opportunity to accentuate the positives in a particular individual or group's life. The term 'strokes' refers to giving somebody a reassuring touch, a hand on the arm, for example. It is often used in a metaphorical sense to refer to anything we can say or do that will be geared towards boosting somebody's confidence. This is an important activity to undertake because people embroiled in problems can often lose sight of the bigger picture, as we have discussed earlier. People who are worried or anxious can understandably see nothing but the negatives at times. They can feel deskilled and devalued. Giving people positive strokes – that is, pointing out their strengths, abilities and positives – can have a tremendous benefit, but it has to be done carefully.

Simply stating positives in a mechanistic or unfeeling way is not likely to help. It will come across to the person or persons concerned as if you are simply following a mechanical routine or technique. It will have the effect of distancing you from people and can thus potentially be very counterproductive. Positive strokes need to be given genuinely, with warmth. They need to be based on a genuine concern for helping this particular individual to appreciate his or her strengths and to feel better about the situation they face. Blandly uttering positives in a random way will not help. It needs to be part of a skilful process of engaging with the people concerned, showing a genuine concern for the problem they face, but seeking to balance the anxieties they have against the strengths and positives they bring to the situation. This has to be done in a way that is not patronizing or belittling.

Sometimes this can be achieved by the careful use of questions. For example, instead of simply saying: 'I think you are good at x', questions can be asked which lead the individual concerned to conclude that he or she is good at x. Practice focus 2.8 illustrates this.

In addition to using positive strokes appropriately ourselves, we can help other people to do so – for example, where somebody is responsible for the well-being of another person (this could be a parent in a family or a supervisor in a workplace). Problems and tensions may be arising because of the lack of positive strokes. It could therefore be very beneficial, in some circumstances, to help certain people to appreciate the benefits of positive strokes and perhaps even to teach them how to use them appropriately (although you have to feel fairly confident in using this technique yourself before you can realistically start teaching it to others).

One important point to consider is timescales. In some situations, positive strokes can make an almost instant improvement in the situation. In other circumstances, it may take longer. For example, in a situation where there are entrenched, long-term problems, the use of positive strokes is not likely to have an immediate impact. It may take a while for positive strokes (and other interventions) to undermine the culture of negativity, defeatism and cynicism that is so often associated with entrenched problems.

Practice focus 2.8

Lisa had got to the point where she was despairing about being able to sort her problems out. She felt worn down, deskilled and largely incapable. Reba was keen to help her but was beginning to feel overwhelmed by the strong sense of negativity she was getting from Lisa. She decided that she would need to inject some degree of positivity into the situation if she was going to be able to make progress in helping Lisa. She therefore decided to spend some time looking at what Lisa had going for her – what her strengths were. She thought of using a SWOT analysis, but felt Lisa was too demotivated to go along with that. She therefore decided to try positive strokes by using questions:

Reba: What do you see as your strengths?

Lisa: What strengths? What are you talking about?

Reba: Well for a start, wouldn't you say you are a good mother?

Lisa: Oh yes, I've always put my children first.

Reba: Well, that strikes me as not just one strength, but a whole set of strengths, wouldn't you say?

Lisa: I suppose so.

Reba: Right. So let's see, what other strengths are there we can identify? . . .

Providing an anchor
Providing security in times of instability

Sometimes people go through some very difficult circumstances with perhaps an accumulation of events adding pressure upon pressure, with the result that the people experiencing all this feel that they are under siege. Sometimes the situation can involve major losses, such as the death of somebody close to you, and this can be exacerbated by other problems arising at around the same time. Consequently, what is often necessary is for people to 'ride the storm'. What I mean by this is that, in many sets of circumstances, there is not going to be an easy short-term answer. It is going to take time to unravel the problems even though the individuals concerned may be in great distress and experiencing great pain in the process. Sometimes we have to acknowledge this by making it clear to people that we cannot take their pain away, but we can try to be with them while they go through it. Indeed, simply being with someone while they experience such difficulties can be an important steadying influence upon them – perhaps especially with young people who are likely to have less experience of having encountered such situations.

To some people this may sound sentimental, but it is a reality. When people are having to ride the storm, knowing that there is somebody there who is offering moral support at least can be of tremendous value. This is what is meant by anchoring.

I use this term to refer to situations where people may feel that they are in very stormy seas and in danger of being completely overwhelmed or washed away. The idea of an anchor is that it cannot stop the seas from being stormy. It cannot take away the worries and the difficulties, but it can provide some degree of stability and support. It can provide some sense of holding on to get through the difficult times. In some situations, this anchor role could be the difference between somebody coping and not coping, or 'going under'. I once received a thank you card from a student. I was surprised by this as I had not done anything to help her other than simply to listen carefully to her on two or three occasions when she had come to see me about the terrible times she was going through at home. When I asked her about why she had sent me the card, she said it was because having those little chats with me gave her an anchor. She felt that she got through that very difficult situation without giving up the course because she knew there was at least one person there who was willing to listen and to offer support.

On many occasions, we will be the ones who are called upon to be anchors for other people. As problem solvers, we are the ones who will be seeking to ensure that, while we may not be able to resolve certain difficulties, we can at least provide some sense of stability and anchoring through the stormy seas. However, there may be times when we need an anchor ourselves, and it is an important self-care skill to think about who could fulfil that role for us if we needed it.

In addition, anchoring can be something that we can teach others to do. For example, many people feel very anxious when they are alongside people who are distressed, and have a tendency to back off (this is especially the case when somebody is grieving). While this sense of helplessness is understandable, the result can be very unhelpful. If somebody backs away from another person they care about who is expressing pain or distress, then that apparent rejection can often add to the sense of pain and distress. From time to time we may therefore be called upon to help somebody to deal with their own feelings of anxiety about supporting somebody else, perhaps by making it clear that, at the moment, it is the other person who has the greater need and so we should try to make sure that our own feelings do not prevent their distress from being recognized and addressed.

Practice focus 2.9

Salif had done very well on his course and he was looking forward to building on the learning he had achieved. He felt confident he would do well in his career. However, there was one thing he felt uncomfortable about, namely his feelings of unease when dealing with people who were expressing high levels of emotion – particularly people who were grieving. His supervisor had emphasized the importance of being an 'anchor' for people when they needed it, but Salif knew that this was something that did not come easily to him. He worried that he might back away and protect his own feelings at a time when somebody needed him to 'attend', just to be present and not abandon them. However, he was determined not to let this happen and wanted to get enough experience of dealing with such issues to make him feel confident to see them through without backing off.

Pushing the buttons
Acting as an advocate

Power is an important issue in people work, partly because power relations (or at least the abuse of them) are often a source of problems. Similarly, the use of power is often part of the solution that is needed. If we think of power not in a narrow sense of something that you either have or do not have (depending on your position in society or in the organization concerned), but rather as a broader issue in terms of the ability of individuals and groups to influence others and to influence outcomes, then we can see that power is indeed a very relevant topic to people work. Indeed, much of our work as people problem solvers is around influencing others, either influencing the people we are trying to help directly or influencing others who have a bearing on the problem situation.

Pushing the buttons is a term I use to refer to the role of the people worker in trying to make things happen on behalf of the person they are trying to help. In some contexts, but not all, this would be referred to as advocacy. Acting as an advocate for somebody means drawing on your position of power to help them because their own position of power is such that they are not in a position to influence outcomes in the same way as you are. For example, if your position in society or within a specific organization is such that you are likely to be more respected than the person you are trying to help, then that can give you an extra degree of influence. An important notion here is what is known as the hierarchy of credibility. This refers to the fact that the higher somebody is in an organization (or indeed in society itself) the more likely that person is to be heard. Pushing the buttons refers to those situations where your position of authority, trust or respect can be brought to bear in a way that has positive influence on the outcomes you are trying to achieve. For example, a manager may be able to resolve difficulties within a team that individual members of that team are not in a position to tackle. This can also apply outside an employing organization. For example, a patient who is anxious because he or she feels the doctor is not listening to concerns being raised may find that when a nurse raises these concerns with the doctor, they are listened to.

In an ideal world advocacy would not be required as people, regardless of their position in society, would be listened to and their concerns taken seriously. However, the reality is that it is often the case that people find themselves in difficulties and despair at finding a way out because they do not have the power to influence aspects of the situation that need to change. You, as a professional worker, however, may be in a much stronger position to try and influence those factors.

Although 'pushing the buttons' can be very beneficial when used appropriately in the right circumstances, it also has dangers associated with it:

- If we are not careful, advocacy can create a sense of dependency. If we are helpful in one situation it may give the wrong message, namely that we can resolve other matters too.
- If we are not sufficiently skilful in the use of this technique, we may get a backlash that affects the position of the person we are trying to help. For example, if we are tactless in trying to influence a situation, we may create ill-feeling if we alienate the people we are trying to influence. This may have unfortunate consequences in so far as that person may then adopt an even more negative approach to the person we are trying to help.
- We must be careful not to allow the use of power to go to our heads. I have come across situations where people have overstepped the mark and gone beyond using their position of power as a constructive tool to create a positive outcome and have thus strayed into the territory of abusing their power.
- We may set a precedent – that is, if you are very successful in helping one person resolve their difficulties through pushing the buttons, then you may find that others want the same help, even though, in their circumstances, it may not be entirely appropriate.

- The use of advocacy may bring you into conflict with other people who perhaps have a vested interest in the situation remaining as it is. As indicated above, pushing the buttons is about the appropriate use of power. You may therefore find that you enter into positions where other people are using their power against you. Consequently, you will have to be confident that you are sufficiently skilled and experienced to deal with any conflict issues that arise, or you will need to satisfy yourself that you have sufficient backup from your colleagues and/or line manager to deal with any issues that may arise.

Pushing the buttons is clearly a potentially very effective tool but, as I have suggested, it is one that can also go wrong if we are not careful. If you are not already experienced in using this approach, I would encourage you to consider it and to explore in more detail what is involved in the process (see Part Three, 'Guide to further learning'). It is sad that many people who are trying to tackle people problems adopt a very narrow focus and concentrate solely on working directly with the individual or individuals concerned to make progress when it is often the case that change needs to occur elsewhere in order to facilitate progress. Pushing the buttons is just one way of trying to make sure that we adopt a broader focus, one that is more compatible with the complexities of people work.

REBT
Understanding anger

REBT stands for rational emotive behavioural therapy, but do not be put off by this rather grand-sounding term. It is actually relatively straightforward and, when used appropriately, can be very helpful. REBT is an approach associated with the work of Ellis (1962). It was originally called rational therapy, then was changed to rational emotive therapy and, later, to rational emotive behaviour therapy or REBT for short.

REBT is based on another three initials, namely ABC. The theory argues that most people work on an A C model and miss out the B. Let us look, then, in a little more detail at what A, B and C stand for.

A stands for activating event. It can be an event or behaviour that triggers off a particular reaction in us. It can refer to an actual event (for example, somebody treating us badly at a particular moment) or to a memory of that event which triggers off a reaction in us.

C stands for consequence. Activating events will have consequences – that is, they will provoke a reaction. For example, referring back to the instance given above of somebody treating us badly, we may react to this angrily.

B refers to beliefs. Beliefs or cognitions are important elements that stand between activating events and consequences or reactions. REBT teaches us that we should beware of the common mistake of assuming that a trigger produces a reaction without there having been any cognitive process in between. To stick with the same example, if I react angrily to somebody treating me badly, then it is because I believe that I should not be treated badly. However, if my belief system were such that I did not have any such notion that I should not be treated badly, then I would not react with anger.

This is a very important theory that can be used as a most helpful tool. This is because unhelpful reactions will often arise as a result of irrational beliefs (B). For example, if I have the irrational belief that no one should refuse requests I make, then I am likely to react inappropriately on the occasion of somebody quite reasonably refusing the request I make. The problem thus can be seen to arise from my irrational belief.

This approach is widely used in anger management. It is used to show that a great deal of anger arises from our belief systems and, in particular, when those belief systems include irrational beliefs. To control anger, then, is not simply a matter of counting to ten, but rather of identifying what are the beliefs that trigger off an angry response and establishing whether or not they are reasonable and realistic in the circumstances.

However, anger management is not the only use for REBT. For example, it can be used to help boost self-esteem. If you have somebody whose belief systems include a belief that they are of little worth or value as a human being, then their reactions are likely to reinforce that view. What often occurs is a vicious circle in which a belief of one's own lack of value (B) results in actions (C) that then reinforce the notion that the person concerned has little worth. Practice focus 2.10 illustrates this.

REBT can be used as a form of self-awareness. For example, if something produces a strong emotional response in me, I can look at my belief systems to identify which of my beliefs or values has been offended. I can then ask myself whether that is a reasonable or rational view that I am adopting and if not, seek to change that.

REBT can also be used as a therapeutic tool to help others, to review their beliefs and their reactions to situations, especially where there is an identifiable pattern of their reactions causing problems either for themselves, for others or both. For example, if someone reacts very strongly to even the smallest of failures at a particular task, then that can lead to a situation where the tensions and pressures are so high that the situation becomes difficult. It could then pay dividends to look at why this person reacts so strongly to minor failures by identifying what it is within their belief system that is triggering this reaction.

REBT can also be a very helpful tool in working with groups or teams. For example, it can be used as a team development exercise. A team can be asked to identify what its core beliefs and values are and then to see whether they are making reasonable, rational assumptions. It can also be done the other way round – that, is to begin with any problems that they may be experiencing and then try and trace those problems back to the possible inclusion of an irrational belief in their collective team system (or culture).

REBT can be a most effective tool and can be very thought provoking if used appropriately. Of course, it has to be used sensitively, as when we are talking about people's beliefs, we are addressing issues that are very close to home. We have to be very careful that we are not giving people the impression that we are 'psychoanalysing' them. We have to be sufficiently skilful in our use of this technique to make sure that it does not come across as intrusive.

Practice focus 2.10

Sian was the manager of a busy team that was under constant pressure. She made sterling efforts to keep things going as best she could in difficult circumstances. However, things went from bad to worse. The demands kept building up and the resources available to meet those demands were shrinking. Sian became increasingly stressed and felt she could not continue any longer. She therefore told her supervisor that she was considering leaving and taking up a less demanding job. Her supervisor was very concerned about this as she did not want to lose

Sian, since she was an excellent manager for the most part. Sian's supervisor talked to her in depth about the situation and was able to identify that Sian had an irrational belief that, despite increasing demands and shrinking resources, she should be able to maintain both the quality and quantity of the team's work. This irrational belief meant that Sian was not looking at alternative strategies for managing a situation of work overload – instead she was just working harder and harder and driving herself and her team into the ground. Her supervisor helped her to realize that she had to learn how to let go of the idea that she could achieve the impossible.

The RED approach
Managing conflict

This is a tool I have developed that has proven to be a helpful method to use in the work I undertake around conflict management issues. Situations involving conflict tend to have a high level of tension associated with them. It can therefore be very helpful to have a clear systematic framework to adopt when dealing with conflict. It can help to create a greater sense of confidence and trust and thus dissipate some of the tension.

The RED approach can be broken down into its three component parts. **R** stands for *recognize* the conflict. This is an important point to emphasize for two reasons. First, there is a strong tendency for people to feel uncomfortable about conflict issues and perhaps to brush them under the carpet where possible, to hope that they will go away if they are ignored. Of course, that is a dangerous tactic and often leads to conflicts festering over time and therefore getting worse. Second, people may not recognize conflict because it is a much more common entity than most people realize. What they see as ordinary, everyday behaviour will often be based on an underlying conflict that is not being brought out into the open. For example, it may not be recognized that somebody's non-cooperation in a particular project is due to conflict between that person and one or more others who are also involved in it. As we noted in relation to 'PCS analysis', it is very easy to individualize the situation and regard such a person as being awkward or difficult rather than appreciate the wider context, which may have a lot to do with conflict. The first step towards dealing with conflicts, therefore, is to recognize where and when they occur.

E stands for *evaluate* the conflict. It would not be realistic for us to attempt to resolve every conflict we encounter – they are just so widespread. However, it is also dangerous to ignore significant conflicts, as they are likely to get worse rather than better if not addressed. The key task, therefore, is to evaluate conflicts, to weigh them up, so that we get an idea of how important or significant they are, how detrimental their consequences could be if allowed to develop, how likely or otherwise escalation of the conflict is, and so on. To a large extent, this involves using the assessment skills discussed in *People Skills*. Our ability to evaluate conflict can develop over time through experience and perhaps also through training. The important point to note is that we should not leave such matters to chance. We do not have a crystal ball at our disposal, and so we cannot know for sure that a particular conflict will prove very detrimental if not tackled, but there are tools available to us that will enable us to form an opinion as to how significant a particular conflict is (see, for example, the discussion of 'Risk assessment' below).

D stands for *deal* with the conflict. In a limited number of cases, simply being aware of the conflict (and those involved being aware that you know of it) can be sufficient to keep the conflict under control and make it manageable. However, in the majority of cases, it is dangerous to allow significant conflicts to remain live issues. If our evaluation has determined that a particular conflict is significant, then we now have the task of deciding how best to deal with it. There are various options open to us, but all of them are likely to involve some degree of attempting to get the parties to appreciate each other's point of view. Communication is therefore a key part of trying to resolve conflict. Encouraging open and clear communication can be an invaluable part of conflict management.

Handling conflict is a central part of dealing with people problems because it is so often the case that conflict is either the cause, in part at least, of such problems or is, again in part at least, the result of such problems. In tackling conflict issues, it is important to avoid the two destructive extremes. On the one hand, we do not want to fall into the trap of trying to pretend that the conflict is not there. This 'ostrich' approach is doomed to failure, of course. But, despite its dangerousness, it is still a very common reaction to conflict. At the other extreme, we also need to avoid overreaction. A panic reaction to conflict will only 'up the stakes', as it were, by increasing the tensions and thereby increasing the likelihood of a harmful outcome. Maintaining the healthy balance between these two destructive extremes is not always easy. However, it is to be hoped that the RED approach can be a helpful tool in assisting you to try and remain free from the problems associated with these two extremes.

At a personal level, the RED approach can be used to make you confident that you are responding appropriately to a situation characterized by conflict. It can therefore be a significant source of confidence and reassurance. It is likely to be less useful in dealing directly with people who are in conflict, but that is not to rule out its use altogether. As with any tool, the skill of the craftsperson in deciding when it is appropriate and how best to use it is paramount. One arena where it can certainly be helpful, though, is in working with groups of people. It can be used as a means of helping to identify any conflicts or tensions that exist, evaluating them in terms of their relative importance and, where appropriate, coming up with strategies for dealing with them. This can be done in a preventative way – that is, by anticipating conflicts and preparing the ground for preventing them or nipping them in the bud. It can also be used in a remedial way once conflicts have already begun to arise.

Whichever way it is used, the RED approach offers a clear and helpful way of dealing with some very demanding situations that could become major problems if not handled sensitively and appropriately.

Reframing

Redefining problem situations to allow people to move forward

---

This is a tool that has something in common with REBT, as discussed above. The basic idea behind reframing is that sometimes we cannot change the objective circumstances in which we are working or living, but perhaps we can change our attitude towards them. Reframing is based on the psychological concept of 'cognitive restructuring', as Marshall (1998) puts it:

> Cognitive restructuring refers to a way of dealing with a problem where what are seen as acceptable solutions, or outcomes, cannot reasonably be expected. If the conditions cannot be changed then the only way

forward is to change your conceptualisation of them and your own relation to them. This may mean lowering your expectations in some cases.
(p. 25)

Lowering our expectations is one way of achieving this but, of
course, is not the only one. What it is about is renegotiating expectations. This is an important issue in relation to stress, as a very
common cause of stress is either unclear or unrealistic expectations.

There is also a parallel here with assertiveness. It would be a
mistake to see assertiveness (that is, seeking win–win solutions) as
being simply a matter of compromising or reducing expectations. It
is more a case of finding ways forward where both parties can be
happy. Reframing is very similar. It is a way of finding an alternative approach that can be acceptable. I once came across a man who
told me that his job was very stressful because it involved trying to
find resources that were largely absent. He told me that his job was
necessarily stressful because failure was an inherent part of his
job. He was being asked to find resources that, in his view, did not
exist. However, when I suggested that he should check and, if
necessary, renegotiate his job description to make sure that it
stated words to the effect that his job was to *look for* rather than
find such resources, he was delighted with my comments. It gave
him a way forward. By reframing his job description in this small
but significant way, it changed it from being a job necessarily characterized by failure to one that could involve success. That is, if his
job was to look for resources, he could still do an excellent job even
though he might not find such resources, as that could be due to
factors beyond his control.

Reframing can also be linked to pessimism and optimism.
Sometimes reframing is needed because somebody is being unduly
negative or unduly positive (in reality, the former tends to be more
likely than the latter). Somebody who is prone to a pessimistic
outlook may need help in reframing things in a more positive way
while somebody who has an optimistic outlook may, on occasion,
need help with reframing to be more realistic about what can be
achieved in the circumstances or what outcomes can be expected.
An example of positive reframing would be, 'I only managed to get
it right three times out of five' being changed into 'I managed to get
it right most of the time'. An example of reframing to move somebody away from an unrealistic version of optimism might be, 'we

are bound to get this contract' being changed to 'we're in with a good chance of getting this contract'.

The technique can be used directly and explicitly. For example, we can say to somebody, 'I think it would be helpful if we reframed the situation' and then explain what we mean by that. Alternatively, we may do it implicitly. For example, when someone talks to us in a way that we feel is in need of reframing, we can feed it back to that person in a more realistic way. For example, if someone says: 'I don't know anything about that sort of thing', then a useful reply could be, 'I take it by that that you mean you will need training before undertaking this role and we would certainly want you to undertake such training'. In a way, this is a form of gentle challenging and indeed this is often what is required – a way of challenging something that needs reframing (see the discussion above of elegant challenging). Such challenging can be done in a variety of ways – for instance, a counter example can be given. If someone says: 'Nobody has ever managed to do that', then this can be challenged by the response of 'What about Sarah – didn't she do that?'

Naming the process, as discussed above, can also be used to good effect. If someone is being too self-centred about a particular issue, this can be gently challenged by 'We always seem to be coming back to the implications for you and I can see why that's important, but I think we have to look at the bigger picture here in terms of the implications for everybody concerned'.

Reframing is also something that can apply to groups of people or teams. It may be, for example, that one source of conflict is that different people within a group are conceptualizing the same issues in different ways and, in order to reach some sort of workable consensus, it will be necessary to come up with a shared reframing of the issues. Coming up with such a shared reframing may be a long and difficult job, but it can be one that is well worth the time and effort invested in it if it means that a team or group of people can move forward away from problems they have been experiencing.

Some people in the past have been a little cynical about reframing and see it as a form of cheating or self-delusion: 'If you can't have what you want, just kid yourself into believing you never wanted it anyway'. However, this is a gross oversimplification of what reframing is all about. As REBT has taught us, how we react to events in our lives will depend not only on those particular events but on our beliefs about them and about ourselves. This is what is known as a phenomenological perspective – that is, one that emphasizes the importance of perception and meaning. Often, such perceptions are based on habit (see 'The three Hs') and when we examine those habits, we may well be prepared to change our perspective. For example, if someone who has worked with children for many years were to move to a job that involved working with adults, then there may be a number of ways in which he or she would need to adjust. There may be habits that have developed over the years that are quite appropriate in working with children but which need to be reframed when working with adults.

Recognizing grief
Appreciating the significance of loss and grief

Loss and grief are significant aspects of human experience. They can have a drastic effect on our lives, perhaps when we least expect it. The fact that the word 'bereavement' means 'robbed' gives us some idea of how emotionally significant loss can be.

A major loss can affect us in the following ways:

- *Thoughts* It is not uncommon for people who have experienced a major loss to find it difficult to 'think straight'. They may be dominated by thoughts about what has happened and may therefore lose sight of other important issues.
- *Feelings* It perhaps goes without saying that our emotions will be significantly affected by a major loss. The emotional reaction can vary enormously depending on the circumstances (and the individual concerned), but a very common reaction is for the intense feelings generated to go either inwards (as depression and guilt, for example) or outwards (as anger or even aggression).
- *Actions* Our behaviour can change dramatically as a result of loss. We can behave in ways that are out of character (a form of stress response, in effect). Our behaviour can also be unreliable – a drop in work performance, or even actions that are actually dangerous (neglectful operation of machinery, for example).

The three of these can combine to make a major impact on our relationships (and, indeed, other aspects of our lives). This can produce a very dangerous situation in which our experience of loss can put a major strain on relationships (especially where the loss has also affected the others involved in those relationships), thus putting those relationships at risk of breaking down, thereby adding further to the pressures being experienced and creating a situation where a grieving person loses support at the time they need it most.

There are two important points to emphasize about loss:

1. Although loss and grief are closely associated with death, we should not fall into the trap of concentrating on death-related losses only. Loss can occur in a variety of ways that are not linked to a death – for example, the breakdown of a relationship, the loss of a status or position, and the loss of opportunities or aspirations. If we draw too close a link between loss and death, we run the risk of missing a significant range of loss issues that are unconnected with death.

2. Different people react to loss in different ways. There is no standard, 'one size fits all' approach to grief. This is an important point to recognize because, if we do not take this message on board, we may find ourselves in a position where we are putting somebody under pressure to grieve in a particular way (in accordance with our own views of what constitutes 'healthy' grieving) that they do not feel comfortable with. This could amount to kicking somebody when they are down.

When we consider the two points above in combination, we can see that we have a situation where grief can often go unacknowledged because (i) if the loss is not death related, it may not register with us that we are dealing with a loss situation; and (ii) if we do not recognize certain thoughts, feelings or actions as being grief related (because they do not fit the stereotype of 'the grieving person'), it again may not register that we are dealing with loss issues. Consider the following examples:

*   A woman who has worked in the same place for over twenty years is transferred to a new location. Normally highly motivated, she becomes withdrawn and lethargic after the move.
*   A man becomes distant and distracted after his daughter leaves home to move in with her boyfriend.

- A couple become very aggressive towards one another after their close friends move away.
- A child begins to behave in a very disruptive and challenging way after being sexually abused.

The list could go on – loss (and our reactions to it) is much more common than most people realize. Consequently, it is possible for us to fail in our attempts to help people tackle their problems because we do not recognize the significance of loss and grief. In Part One above I emphasized the importance of 'problem identification' – that is, being clear about what the problem is before we attempt to tackle it. It is important that we should consider loss issues when identifying problems. If we do not, then there is clearly the danger that we will not be aware of key issues and our efforts to help could be wasted or, in certain circumstances, could do harm.

It is often the case that people who are grieving as a result of losses that are not death related do not realize the effect that grieving is having on them. For example, someone may become depressed without making a connection between their state of mind and their loss. Recognizing grief and its significance in our lives is therefore an important tool for us to use in dealing with a wide variety of problem situations.

It is something we need to consider in terms of how we make sense of situations and how we respond to them. It is also something we need to consider in terms of how we help others understand, and face up to, the problems they are experiencing. For example, making someone aware that their current situation may be largely due to an unrecognized grief reaction can, if handled sensitively and appropriately, be a huge step in helping people move forward. It is an example of 'catharsis', the freeing up of emotional blockages that can be preventing us from dealing with our problems.

Much the same can happen on a collective basis (families, teams, members of particular groups and so on). Indeed, there can be shared grief responses that can be very powerful influences on the actions of individuals within groups and on group dynamics.

Of course, loss and grief issues need to be handled very sensitively as they can relate to very sore points for people – and that includes us, as problem solvers. We are not immune to the effects of grief so we must make sure that, in dealing with loss and grief, we make sure that we have adequate support to fall back on should issues relating to our own experiences of loss arise.

Responding to feelings
Taking account of the emotional dimension

Emotion is often presented as if it were an exception to the rule, something that represents a change from the normal state of affairs – for example, when somebody says 'when I mentioned the subject, he became emotional'. In reality, everything we do has an emotional dimension. For example, being agitated may be seen as being emotional, but is calmness not an emotion too? It is far too simplistic and misleading to think that life is basically a rational undertaking and that occasionally emotions creep in. Emotions, in one form or another, will affect everything that we do, as there is no neutral, non-emotional state.

This has quite significant implications. It is not just a technical matter of definition of what constitutes emotional and what does not. Rather, it is a case of realizing the profound and far-reaching implications of recognizing that emotions play at least a small part in shaping everything we do. We must therefore move away from the idea that emotions apply only during exceptional circum- stances – for example, when somebody is particularly happy or unhappy. Being neither particularly happy nor particularly unhappy is in itself an emotional state.

The concept of emotional intelligence is one that has become quite popular in some areas, even though the concept itself is quite confusing, as the notion of emotion does not sit easily with that of intelligence. But, terminology aside, the point that it is important to recognize and respond appropriately to feelings is an extremely significant one, and that, after all, is the basic tenet of emotional intelligence. To many in the people professions, emotional intelli- gence is old wine in new bottles, in the sense that the importance of recognizing feelings (our own and those of the people we are working with) and responding appropriately to them is an idea that has a much longer history and much firmer foundations than the relatively new notion of emotional intelligence.

An important part of responding to feelings, particularly the feelings of others, is to be able to read body language. This is some- thing we can practise. When we have some spare time we can watch other people and think about what emotions they are indi- cating through their non-verbal communication and how precisely this is done. For example, we can look at how closely people stand in relation to each other and work out whether this reflects the closeness of the relationship. We can also look at such matters as eye contact. The more we develop these observation skills, the more skilful at reading body language we can become. We can do this in live action, as it were, by watching people in our ordinary lives, but we can also do the same through television and film. Indeed, in these latter examples, body language is sometimes exaggerated for dramatic effect in order to make a point to ensure that viewers do not miss out on a crucial part of the story line. This means that TV and film can be particularly useful at highlighting the relationship between body language and emotion.

The other side of this coin is that we need to make sure that our body language is appropriate. What type of emotional message are we trying to convey in the way we use non-verbal communication? This can be at a very simple level (for example, are we showing interest through smiling?) or at much more complex and intricate levels. The more aware we become over time of these important issues, the more skilful we can become at making sure that we are using body language appropriately and not giving people the wrong message. For example, you may be very interested in what some-body is trying to say and very keen to help them, but if your anxiety leads you to refrain from making eye contact, the actual message you may be giving in emotional terms is that you do not care, that you are not prepared to engage with this person.

Of course, a key part of emotional response is being able to understand and identify our own feelings. This is a matter of self-awareness. How much do you know about what makes you tick emotionally? How tuned in are you to what pleases you, what annoys you, what enthuses you, what turns you off, and so on? This is not a recommendation that you should psychoanalyse yourself, but rather a plea for a major focus on self-awareness. It is unreal-istic to expect to be able to respond appropriately to other people's emotions if we have not got a clue about our own.

It is important to be able to respond to other people's emotions in a constructive way. This means being able to reinforce positive emotions. For example, if somebody is commenting on how their confidence is beginning to grow, then this is something we can encourage further. However, if somebody is expressing destructive emotions, our challenge is to be able to respond to those feelings positively and constructively, not by pretending they are not there, nor by reacting inappropriately ourselves. In between those two unhelpful extremes is a constructive and helpful balance. That is what we should aim for. The 'SARAH' approach discussed below can be helpful in this regard, as indeed can some of the other tools here. However, the point remains that a major part of responding appropriately to other people's feelings is to have a certain degree of awareness of the importance of emotions, how they influence individuals and interactions between people or, in short, emotional intelligence.

The right person for the job
Matching skills and aptitudes to task

This can be seen to apply in two ways. First of all, it applies in its usual sense – relating to the workplace and employment matters. A lot of stress can arise because somebody is in the wrong job. That is, their particular employment role at the moment is not suited to their talents, experience or interests (Thompson, 1999). For example, having a creative person in a mundane role that is basically routine and does not require any creativity can be soul destroying for the individual concerned, whereas having somebody who enjoys the security and structure of routine, mundane work, may feel very threatened in a job that requires creativity and reflective practice.

This is a matter of selection and recruitment as well as job design. Any good manager will know that trying to fit a square peg into a round hole is asking for trouble. Care therefore needs to be taken to ensure that people being asked to undertake particular tasks are the best people to do so in the circumstances. We should be very wary of a blanket approach that assumes that any competent individual should be capable of any task. Life is, of course, not that simple.

While the employment issues related to the notion of the right person for the job are clearly important, we should not neglect the other side of the coin when it comes to people problem solving. Helping people to solve their problems often involves asking individuals to undertake particular tasks or to fulfil certain roles. We can therefore apply the same logic and look at who is the best person for the job, who is the best person to undertake a particular role or to complete a particular task within a problem-solving framework. For example, in a fraught, volatile situation that requires calm, it would be wise to entrust certain tasks or duties to the person or persons within the problem situation who appear to be the most stable, calm and collected. At the other extreme, if we were to ask somebody who is easily excitable to undertake certain roles, this may lead to a counterproductive situation where his or her actions actually increase the level of instability and concern rather than reduce tensions and anxiety.

Another implication of this is that we should be careful not to set people up to fail. For example, if we are dealing with somebody with a low level of confidence who is very anxious about particular aspects of their life or work situation, then it could be disastrous to ask that person to do something that involves a lot of confidence or even courage. Simply encouraging or cajoling somebody to do something that they feel they are unable to do is not only insufficient, it can actually be very unhelpful indeed as it may undermine that person's confidence still further.

A positive approach can be based on first of all mapping or scanning the situation, working out what needs doing, and then moving along to look at who is the best person for each of the items that have been identified from this scan. We should, of course, not seek to impose our view on other people as that, in itself, can be unhelpful, but rather to try and positively influence developments in the right direction. Often the people we are seeking to help will have enough self-awareness to know that they are not cut out for certain jobs, or are keen to adopt certain jobs, as the case may be. However, at times, certain individuals may volunteer for tasks that they are not suited for. This is clearly a situation that will need to be handled sensitively and carefully. It will require us to draw on our interpersonal skills.

Finding the right person for the job does not have to be a duty that falls solely to you. It is something that, in many circumstances, can be done collectively. There can be group discussion about who is the best person to undertake particular tasks or fulfil certain roles. Do not make the mistake of assuming that it is all down to you individually.

In summary, the idea of the right person for the job can be seen as something to consider as part of our assessment – are the problems being experienced, in part at least, due to somebody undertaking roles or duties that they are not well suited to or feel uncomfortable with? It can also be an important part of our intervention – that is, as a problem-solving tool in its own right. Even if the problem situation does not derive from an inappropriate allocation of job roles, reallocating may, none the less, be an important part of the solution or a step towards finding the solution.

Risk assessment
Analysing the risks involved in a given situation
_____

More or less everything we do in life involves a degree of risk. Even if we play things safe and try to keep risks to a minimum, we run the risk of missing out on some important opportunities (perhaps opportunities to solve problems we have been wrestling with for quite some time). Risk, then, is not something we can avoid altogether – it is something we have to learn to manage. Or to be more accurate, it is something that we need to manage *better,* as basic risk management is something that we can all do (it is something we learn as part of growing up), even though some people may be better at it than others.

Risk management is something we do in an informal way every day of our lives. When we are crossing the road, we are weighing up whether it is safe to do so, making a judgement about the speed of vehicles, the time it will take us to get across the road and so on. For most of the risks we take, this informal approach based on years of experience is perfectly adequate. However, there will come times where we need a more formal approach – one where we explicitly identify the risk factors we are dealing with, partly to make sure we have considered them carefully and are fully aware of them and partly to make sure we have a record of them for the benefit of others in the future (for example, a colleague trying to tackle the same issues in helping someone and therefore facing the same – or similar – risks as those you faced and explored carefully).

A key part of risk management is having a clear picture of the risks you (and the people you are seeking to help) face and their implications. This is where risk assessment comes in. There are various approaches to risk assessment, but one I have found particularly helpful is the Brearley model. Paul Brearley (1982) developed his model by exploring the risks faced by older people living in the community. However, his model has been adapted to apply in a wide variety of settings and is now recognized as a generic risk assessment tool. It can be summarized as follows:

1. Begin by considering the *context* you are working in. Are there, for example, any cultural differences that may influence how you interpret the situation or how you respond to it?

2. Identify the *dangers*. A danger is what you want not to happen. That is, if there is a loose stair carpet, the danger is that someone will fall down the stairs and be injured or even killed.

3. Identify the *hazards*. These are the risk factors that will make the danger more likely to occur (in the above example, the loose stair carpet would be a significant hazard). Other common hazards may be the influence of alcohol (people are at more risk when they are drunk), the use of machinery, someone having a 'short fuse' and being prone to violence, and so on.

4. Divide the hazards into *two types:* situational and predisposing. Situational hazards are those which relate to the specific circumstances at the moment. For example, the stair carpet is not normally loose, but has become loose because the tacks holding it in place have worn away over time. Situational hazards are therefore related to specific time periods. Predisposing hazards, by contrast, are the ones that persist over time. They relate to particular predispositions (for example, Alan's tendency to run up the stairs). It may be the case that he has been running upstairs for years but has never had an accident. However, the combination of a situational hazard (the loose stair carpet) with a predisposing one (his tendency to run up the stairs) may well be what produces the danger – the actual accident of Alan falling down the stairs.

5. Identify the *strengths*. What aspects of the situation make it less likely that the danger will occur? What are the counterbalancing features? For example, if you have someone who is prone to violence (predisposing hazard) in a situation of high tension (a situational hazard), the combination of the two may be potentially explosive. However, there may be other factors (the strengths) that tilt the balance against the danger occurring (for example, someone present who has skills in defusing fraught situations, someone with aggression prevention skills).

6. Identify *gaps* in your knowledge. What do you *not* know about the situation? Is there anything that could significantly change the situation that you are not aware of? Considering these issues will help to prevent us from making decisions that we may later regret because we acted too soon without first trying to fill some of the gaps in our knowledge. Sometimes the situation is so

dangerous that we have to act without the luxury of gathering extra information or delving into the situation further, but even then, being aware of what gaps there are in our knowledge could be helpful – for example, by warning us about which aspects of the situation need extra caution.

7. Consider what *actions* are needed. This means that risk assessment is not just about gathering information – it also involves making sense of that information and developing a realistic action plan based on it.

This is, of course, not a foolproof approach to risk assessment, but it does give a very useful framework and structure to work to. I have used it many times and have found it useful both for clarifying my own thinking and for giving the person(s) I am trying to help a degree of confidence and security in what I am doing.

In what circumstances can it be used? Well, it can be drawn upon in basically any situation which involves sufficient risk to justify a formal approach. The precise circumstances will vary from setting to setting and situation to situation, but the key indicator is: sufficient concern to warrant looking closely and explicitly at the risks involved in the situation concerned.

Role reversal
Seeing the situation from someone else's point of view

It is often the case that people who are experiencing problems become so engrossed in the challenges they face, and the anxiety that so often accompanies them, that they do not take account of other dimensions of the situation or of key issues. This tendency to adopt a narrow, partial view is a recurring theme in dealing with people problems, although we should not be surprised by this, as the pressures involved can often prevent people from thinking clearly or looking at the wider picture.

One way of tackling this is through role reversal. This can be done in one of two ways, directly or indirectly. By directly I mean situations where people actually carry out another person's duties. For example, in a situation of conflict, it may pay dividends to ask each of the two parties to undertake the other's role for a limited period (although this may have to be closely supervised to prevent one or both of them sabotaging the other's work). In this way each party can be helped to understand the pressures the other faces and to begin, perhaps, to see the situation from their point of view.

However, situations where this direct approach may be used are likely to be fairly limited, which brings us to the indirect use of role reversal. This involves enabling the benefits of direct role reversal to be achieved through discussion. This can be two separate discussions (one with party A and the other with party B) to try and get each one of them to appreciate the other's point of view or, if you have the skills and confidence to do so, one joint discussion involving both parties where you enable them to explore each other's perspective. This is very close to what happens in the process of mediation as a form of dispute resolution.

One interesting approach to role reversal is what has come to be known as 'Garfinkeling'. This refers to the work of the sociologist Harold Garfinkel who was interested in the 'unwritten' rules of particular societies (the assumptions that go to make up core elements of a culture). According to Garfinkel (1967), we can identify these very important unwritten rules by breaking them – and we can break them by a process of reversal. For example, if we consider unwritten social rules about gender roles, we can identify these rules by reversing the gender. Morgan (1997) makes apt comment when he makes the point that:

> Garfinkel elucidates our taken-for-granted skills by showing us what happens if we deliberately attempt to disrupt normal patterns of life. Look a fellow subway passenger in the eye for a prolonged period of time. He or she will no doubt look away at first but get increasingly uncomfortable as your gaze continues. Perhaps he [sic] will eventually inquire what's wrong, change seats or get off at the next stop. Behave in your neighbor's house as if you live there. Disrupt the smooth and continuous line of your walk down a crowded street with a series of random stops and turns or with the shifty manner of a suspicious character. In each case, you will gradually discover how life within a given culture flows smoothly only insofar as one's behaviour conforms with unwritten codes. Disrupt these norms and the ordered reality of life inevitably breaks down. (p. 139)

Another example would be rules about how people address one another in a power relationship. For example, if Lyn is used to addressing her line manager as Mr Davies, while he calls her Lyn, imagine how strange (and awkward) it would seem, if she called him by his first name or how unfriendly it would seem if he addressed her by her title and surname. Switching things round in this way helps us to realize that unwritten rules are operating and that we are making assumptions – assumptions which may be part of the problem we are trying to solve or which may be acting as obstacles to solving that problem.

Garfinkeling can be used to inject a note of humour and lighten a tense situation, but it also has a serious role to play in bringing out assumptions that can be problematic. Consider the following dialogue:

Facilitator: Why did Sarah get upset with you?
Paul: I don't know.
Facilitator: What did she say to you?
Paul: She said I had sexually harassed her.
Facilitator: And you feel you didn't?
Paul: No, it was just a bit of fun. I didn't mean anything by it. I thought she'd be flattered. [*Pause*] I don't know why women can't take a joke.
Facilitator: If it was the other way round, if it were women making jokes about men and treating them mainly as sexual objects, as if that were the only thing about them that is important, do you think men would like it?
Paul: Yeah, sure, it would be a laugh.
Facilitator: Really? Even if it were day in day out? Don't you think it would get wearing after a while, particularly if it meant that other strengths you've got get overlooked?
Paul: Yeah, I suppose you've got a point. I hadn't thought about it like that.

This sort of dialogue will not in itself sort out the problem of sexual harassment, but the 'switching' involved in Garfinkeling will have laid the foundations for developing awareness and making the individual concerned think more about his actions and their potentially detrimental effects than would otherwise have been the case.

Role reversal can be used as a way of clarifying your own thinking (If somebody accused me of sexual harassment, how would I react? How would I feel?) and thus broadening it out – putting yourself in someone else's moccasins, as it were. It can also be used to help others, to enable them to appreciate other people's perspectives, and it can even be used as a development tool for teams or groups – to promote partnership working by encouraging and supporting people in seeing the situation from other people's point of view.

The effective use of role reversal involves careful planning. It is not a tool that should be used unthinkingly, as it can complicate matters significantly. For example, if it is used in a situation of hostility, it could heighten the hostility if one party chooses to use it as a weapon against the other. Like any tool, role reversal only works where it is used in the appropriate circumstances and with the appropriate skill.

SARAH
Coping with emotional intensity

This is a tool designed to help people deal with raised levels of emotion. Sometimes people problem solvers can feel ill-equipped when they encounter a degree of emotional intensity. This tool is presented as a useful, structured way of trying to make sure that you respond in a positive and helpful manner.

SARAH is an acronym introduced by Lambert (1996b) who argues that: 'When things start to go off the rails and signs of roused emotions appear, think SARAH' (p. 37). SARAH can be explained as follows.

S – *stop talking*   This emphasizes the importance of *listening*. If, for example, someone is becoming agitated, carrying on talking may make the situation worse, whereas showing that we are listening should help to calm things down by demonstrating that we are taking seriously the concerns of the person concerned.

A – *active listening*   Simply listening is not enough – it needs to be *active* listening. That is, we need to *show* we are listening through our body language. This may be simply a nodding head (don't overdo it!), but can also be conveyed in other subtle ways. It is essential that we make the point loud and clear that we are 'attending' to the person. If we do not, we risk aggravating the situation.

R – *reflect content or feeling*   This involves feeding back some aspect of your understanding of the situation. This may involve paraphrasing a key point that has been made, but it should not be simply a case of 'doing parrot-like imitations', as Lambert puts it

(p. 38). It is a question of making it clear that you have understood (or an opportunity to seek further clarification if you have not understood). Where reflecting feelings it is important not to put words into people's mouths. In particular, you should avoid saying 'I know how you feel' because, of course, you do not know how another person feels. It is much better to say something more neutral like: 'I can understand why you might be annoyed by this situation but . . .'.

A – *act with empathy*   It is important to distinguish between empathy and sympathy. The latter involves sharing feelings with someone (if they are sad, you are sad). Empathy, by contrast, involves recognizing and acknowledging someone's feelings without necessarily feeling them yourself. This distinction is important for two reasons:

1.   If you share the feelings of the various people you seek to help it is only a matter of time before you will become burnt out – overloaded by an excess of negative feelings. For self-care reasons you need to keep a certain distance and not take on board other people's feelings through sympathy.
2.   Sympathy can intensify someone's feelings. For example, if someone is expressing anger about the way a third party has treated them, then if you show that you are angry too, you may unwittingly contribute to an escalation of those feelings.

H – *handle objections*   Lambert sums this up well when he comments that:

> When your calm, sensitive handling of the situation has made it easy for your client to listen to reason again, deal with any objections raised. Always deal with what your client says. Never try to second guess 'what they really mean'. You will almost certainly get it wrong. Even if you were to get it right, you will destroy the belief that you have been listening carefully and with empathy and understanding. (p. 39)

This tool can be used in one-to-one encounters, but is also valuable when dealing with a number of people expressing high levels of emotion. This can be a family context, a team within an organization or indeed any situation involving more than one person. The more people there are involved, the greater the danger that emotions will escalate – with one emotional reaction triggering off another. However, the more demanding the situation is because of the number of people involved, the more useful this tool can be.

It is not expected that people can demonstrate the skills involved in SARAH without the opportunity to practise, but the technique does provide a platform from which skill development can take place over time. An important factor in terms of such skill development can be confidence. Dealing with people displaying high levels of emotion can be very daunting, and so it is not surprising that many people may feel very unconfident about tackling such situations. However, it is important to realize that a lot of very effective problem solving happens because the person trying to help 'weathered the storm' of high emotions and, in so doing, won respect and professional confidence. People are much more likely to trust you and your judgement if they know that you have the skills and courage to weather some emotional storms with them, whereas they are likely have little respect for, or confidence in, someone who shrinks away when emotions are to the fore. There is therefore much to be gained from building on the platform that SARAH provides.

SMART objectives
The importance of having clear goals

In Part One of the book, the importance of systematic practice was emphasized. That is, it was argued that it is important to be clear about what we are trying to achieve, how we intend to achieve it and how we will know when we have achieved it. This involves having clear objectives. If we are not clear about what specific objectives we are aiming for, then we will struggle to know whether or not our work has been successful and we bring it to a conclusion. We will also not be clear about what steps we need to take during our intervention if we are not sure where that intervention is supposed to be taking us. Systematic practice is not a rigid approach that does not allow for change and variation over time but if we are not clear what our objectives are to begin with then, when they change, we will be even more confused. Clarity about objectives is therefore paramount in objective people problem solving.

The SMART approach to objective setting is one that has become quite popular in many quarters. SMART is an acronym:

- Specific;
- Measurable;
- Agreed;
- Realistic; and
- Time bound.

O'Connell (2003) comments that: 'SMART objectives date back to the 1950s and are part of "management by objectives" school credited to Drucker (1954)' (p. 38).

Over the years, there have been slight changes to the use of SMART in terms of what the letters refer to. For example, in some versions of SMART the A stands for achievable rather than agreed. However, there is then an overlap with the R for realistic.

Let us now look in more detail at each of the five specific parts of SMART.

Specific This refers to the need to make sure that our objectives are not too general or vague. For example, if we say that our objective is to help someone or support someone, that is not sufficiently specific for us to be able to work out at the end of the day whether or not we have achieved what we set out to do. While our overall aim may be that of helping or supporting somebody, our objectives need to be more specific under the general aim we are pursuing (namely to help someone). The objective of 'boosting Mark's confidence' is not sufficiently specific, whereas 'boosting Mark's confidence to the point where he can achieve tasks x, y and z unaided' is far better.

Measurable This refers to the need to make sure, as far as possible, that we can measure the progress made. That is, we can clearly identify the actual progress made. The term measurement implies the use of numbers. Where we can realistically attach a number to something, this can be very helpful in determining whether or not we have made the progress we wish to. For example, if we are trying to eradicate or reduce the occurrence of an unacceptable behaviour (aggression, for example) then it can be very helpful to be able to measure the incidence of such behaviour before we intervene and after we have intervened. If a particular unacceptable behaviour is recorded as happening on average five times a day, and a month later we are able to record that it is happening no more than twice a day, then this will tell us that (i) we have made good progress, and (ii) we still have further work to do. Note, however, that not everything is measurable and sometimes it can be very artificial to try and attach a numerical scale to something which does not lend itself to that sort of approach. Attempting to make sure that our objectives are measurable is a worthy pursuit but we should not overdo this to the point of making the use of numbers meaningless in certain circumstances. For example, if our objective is to improve somebody's commitment to a particular role, then it may not be possible to measure progress in any precise way because a numerical scale would not be appropriate in such cases. However, there may be other ways of determining whether or not that goal has been achieved, other ways of showing that success has been reached – for example, recognizing clear signs that the role is being fulfilled appropriately.

Agreed The point has already been made in this book that the best form of change is agreed change. That is, if we try to impose our view on people, we are likely to engender resistance that can be unhelpful if not actually counterproductive. It is important to make sure, then, that we are consulting adequately with key stakeholders in any decision making around the objectives we are working towards. In many cases it is unlikely that somebody will be motivated towards pursuing a particular objective if they have not played a part in determining what it should be.

Realistic 'Nothing succeeds like success' is an important adage to remember. Setting objectives that are realistic can produce a virtuous circle, that is, once the person concerned has achieved that objective, it will motivate them to move on to achieve the next objective. However, if the objectives are unrealistic, then the opposite can occur, a vicious circle. That is, if somebody is given an unrealistic task to achieve and they fail to do so, then they may give up on any future tasks as well. Setting unrealistic objectives is therefore a significant demotivator and can lead to significant problems. We therefore have to be very careful to ensure that the objectives we are setting are realistic in the context in which they are to be pursued.

Time bound It is very easy for objectives to drift, for other priorities to take over and for our initial plans to get lost in a confusing welter of other demands and circumstances. Setting a deadline can help to avoid this. Of course, there is no guarantee of success. Deadlines are often not met, but setting a specific deadline for an objective to be achieved will play a part in motivating people to work towards that objective within the defined timescales. Where no timescale is set then there is a danger that the work to be done will fall to the bottom of the priority list and perhaps be forgotten about in the short term at least. However, in setting timescales, we must remember the R of SMART and make sure that such timescales are realistic. There is no point in setting an unrealistic timescale as that will not help at all.

Like so many other tools, the SMART objectives approach can be used in a variety of ways. It can be used on an individual basis to clarify our thinking and make sure that we are being sufficiently focused in our work. It can also be used to help others to be focused in what they are doing. This could apply in a management setting as part of a supervisory relationship, for example, or it could operate in similar fashion in a variety of other settings where there is a professional working trying to help somebody resolve particular difficulties. The SMART objective framework can be useful in such circumstances to remove confusion and provide a focus for our energies. In my experience, I have found that this sort of focus can be very helpful for people who are either anxious or depressed or both. By providing a clear framework and focus, we can help to reduce the negative feelings that are so often part of the situations we deal with as people problem solvers.

SMART objectives can also be used at a group or team level. When there is a particular project being planned then it can be very useful to apply SMART objectives to the planning and, of course, at a later stage to the review of the project and ultimately to its evaluation at its conclusion.

One final note of caution about the use of SMART objectives: we should not allow the benefits of a focused framework to degenerate into the disbenefits of a rigid approach. It is not uncommon for objectives to change because the circumstances in which we are working change. If the objectives do change, then this should signal that it is time for us to review our SMART approach rather than abandon it. It is relatively easy to look again at our objectives if we feel that the circumstances are dictating that they need to change (for example, because it has become apparent that a particular objective is no longer achievable or appropriate). Equally, we should not hold on to our original SMART plans simply because they have the benefit of being clear and focused. If they are no longer appropriate, then they should be changed. Focus and structure should not be confused with rigidity.

SOLER
Managing interpersonal relations

This is a tool deriving from the work of Gerard Egan, a very well-respected author in the people work arena. He presents SOLER under the heading of 'The Microskills of Attending'. Like SARAH, it is an acronym and, also like SARAH, it is designed to help with face-to-face interactions. Egan captures the basis of SOLER well when he argues that:

> The main point is that an internal mind-set in which you are with a client might well lose its impact if the client does not see this internal attitude reflected in your nonverbal communication. (1994, p. 93)

The technique can be summarized as follows:

- **S** – Face the client *squarely.*
  Posture is an important part of 'engaging' with people. If we adopt a posture that does not give a clear message that we are interested, then we should not be surprised to find that we are having little influence. Facing somebody squarely should not be interpreted as 'squaring up' to someone. Rather, it is a matter of showing interest by avoiding a posture that shows that our attention is not being directed elsewhere.
- **O** – Adopt an *open* posture.
  This reinforces the importance of posture. An open posture should give a clear message that we are not being defensive, nor are we seeking to attack. Egan points out that open can be used literally or metaphorically – literally, as in not having our arms or legs crossed and metaphorically, as in adopting an open attitude towards the person(s) you are engaging with.
- **L** – *Lean* towards the other person where appropriate.
  Leaning forward is another way of showing interest. However, it has to be done selectively. This is because leaning forward too much can come across as intrusive. There is also the danger that it will be seen as something you are doing for effect, rather than a skilled worker using an interpersonal skills tool appropriately.
- **E** – Maintain good *eye* contact.
  Good eye contact should not be equated with constant eye contact – in other words, staring. Indeed, this is an easy

mistake to make, to be so concerned with showing interest that we overdo it and end up staring, with the result that we can come across as threatening or at least as unnerving. Good eye contact basically means balanced eye contact – not too much, not too little.

- **R** – Try to be relatively *relaxed*.

  It is important to remember that your involvement with a particular individual is to help him or her (even though this may indirectly help you in some way), and so you need to give a clear message that you are there to help and can be relied upon to do so. Fidgeting or other signs of nervousness can not only be distracting and irritating, they can also give the message that your needs or your concerns are more important than those of the person you are trying to help.

SOLER can be a useful mnemonic to help us focus on effective communication. We should not underestimate just how important interpersonal interactions tend to be. Indeed, if we are not skilful in this area, then our skills in other respects may be of little use to us. That is, if we are not able to do a good job of getting the basics right, then our advanced level skills (for example, mediation skills in a conflict management situation) are likely to be seriously undermined.

Egan writes from a United States perspective, but he acknowledges that it is important to adopt these guidelines cautiously in multicultural settings. This is an important point to make, as non-verbal communication does vary from culture to culture. However, the fact that he talks about 'North-American culture' in the singular suggests that he is not taking full account of issues of cultural diversity.

Cultural differences can apply at a number of levels. For example, one aspect of culture that is often forgotten is that of class. Sometimes there can be class differences that affect how interactions take place. For example, someone from a middle-class background trying to work with someone from a working-class background may find that there are barriers that need to be overcome.

In my view, SOLER can be useful in its own right as a tool for 'attending', as Egan intended. However, it can also be very useful as a basis for developing self-awareness. To connect with other people in order to engage in problem-solving activities, we need to have a good understanding of how we come across to other people. SOLER can be a helpful means of considering these issues. For example, we can look at how we use posture and eye contact and see how we can come across as 'natural' and relaxed, rather than as wooden or nervous.

We should be looking to move through three stages. The first stage is understandably one where we feel nervous and show it indirectly if not directly. The second stage is where we still feel nervous, but we manage to control it or at least disguise it to a certain extent. The third stage is where we are sufficiently experienced and confident that we no longer feel nervous, although we may still have a heightened level of awareness at times (when we are 'on our toes').

If someone goes into this type of work without first feeling nervous, we may be left wondering whether they appreciate what is involved in what they are doing or just how important it is. Some degree of nervousness is to be expected, then, especially in the early stages of our career in this type of work. SOLER can help us to guard against nervousness getting the better of us.

SWOT analysis

Balancing positives and negatives as an aid to decision making

SWOT analysis is a decision-making tool that has its roots in marketing theory. It was originally developed by the Boston Consulting Group for the purpose of helping companies to make decisions about marketing plans. However, over the years, it has become widely used as a general decision-making tool.

It can be used in a wide variety of situations and settings. It can be used as a framework for informing decisions about plans, developments and projects. It can also be used as a team development tool, for self-analysis (clarification of one's own thinking) or even a tool of intervention in working directly with people experiencing problems.

However, before going into too much detail about how it can be used, we should first examine what is involved in undertaking a SWOT analysis. As Figure 2.8 illustrates, SWOT analysis involves dividing a sheet of paper into four sections by drawing a line across the middle and a line down the middle. The top left-hand corner is

S	W
Knowledge, skills and experience Commitment to quality Good team spirit Sense of humour Supportive manager Access to equipment Good training available	Cramped office – can cause tensions, low morale Work overload – no let up, quality being compromised High staff turnover – difficult to maintain stability/continuity
O	T
Build on positives – promote good morale Plans for moving building may resolve office overcrowding problem	Vicious circle – staff turnover = more work = more staff leave Team may be disbanded as part of planned reorganization – need to stick together Work overload may lead to dangerous mistakes being made

Figure 2.8 SWOT analysis from a team development day

headed 'S' which stands for strengths. The top right-hand corner is headed 'W' which stands for weaknesses. The bottom left-hand corner is headed 'O' which stands for opportunities and the bottom right-hand corner is headed 'T' which stands for threats.

If we look carefully at the resulting framework, what we can note is that the left-hand side of the page focuses on the positives – strengths and opportunities. The right-hand side of the page focuses on negatives – the weaknesses and threats. This is useful because it helps us to provide a balanced overview of the situation we are analysing. Sometimes people are biased in one direction or another. For example, people who are used to dealing with problems may tend to focus on the negative side and pay relatively little attention to the positives. A sales rep, by contrast, may be occupationally inclined to focus on highlighting the positives and playing down the negatives. So, regardless of your occupational background, SWOT analysis should be a useful tool for helping to provide a more balanced approach that takes account of both positives and negatives.

The top half of the diagram can be seen to represent the present (strengths and weaknesses now). The bottom half of the diagram can be seen to represent the future (opportunities and threats for the future). This temporal dimension to the framework is what makes it a useful decision-making tool. It can balance the present situation against likely future outcomes, divided into positives (opportunities) and negatives (threats).

The analysis is carried out by first of all entering the appropriate words in the four boxes. Second, we should look at the resulting outcomes from this in terms of any patterns which emerge. Are there any themes which are giving us warning signs, for example? Are there any positive themes that we can build on and make the most of? In short, what does this overview of strengths, weaknesses, opportunities and threats tell us about the situation we are analysing?

The tool can be used by a single individual to clarify his or her thoughts. For example, you could use SWOT analysis to analyse a particular situation you are currently dealing with and, in so doing, you may obtain a better view of the situation. It is amazing how, by writing words into four boxes on a sheet of paper like this, we can recognize patterns and issues that otherwise may not have become apparent to us.

SWOT analysis can also be used in direct intervention. For example, you could sit down with a particular individual or group of people and ask them to undertake a SWOT analysis of the situation they currently face. This is likely to bring out the negative aspects, fears and problems, for example, but if it is done properly, it should also bring out potential solutions in terms of strengths and opportunities. It is very easy for people who are experiencing problems to adopt a very negative mindset and not take account of positives, thus blocking progress towards potential solutions. SWOT analysis can help to counterbalance this. Of course, it will not solve problems in itself, but it can be a useful tool for helping the individuals concerned to gain greater insight into the situation they face and may point up ways forward.

SWOT analysis can also be used as a management tool – for example, by inviting a group of staff involved in a particular project to undertake an analysis of that project. Once again, this can help to identify strengths to be built on, opportunities to be capitalized on as well as weaknesses to be wary of and threats to avoid or remove.

Similarly, SWOT analysis can be used as part of a team development process. I have used this technique a number of times myself in running team development workshops. I divide teams of staff into sub-groups, issue each sub-group with flipchart and pen and ask them to undertake a SWOT analysis of their particular team. After a while, we place the flipchart papers on the walls of the training room and invite members of the team to circulate and compare notes across the different SWOT analyses that have been produced. In my experience, this often produces a lot of commonality across the different analyses, which helps to reinforce the message that can be deduced from the analysis. However, it can also be very useful when conflicts or differences of perspective between sub-groups emerge and this can identify issues that the team needs to address.

One note of caution about the use of SWOT analysis: in some quarters it has become well established as a working tool. However, this can lead to problems. I have encountered situations where undertaking a SWOT analysis becomes a routine process, and then is simply reduced to a bureaucratic issue rather than a genuine decision-making tool. For example, I recently came across a situation where somebody undertook a SWOT analysis in just a few minutes, recorded the points on paper very briefly, but then passed on to the next part of the process without making any attempt whatsoever to look at what the SWOT analysis told us. SWOT it may have been, analysis it was not.

It is also important to note that SWOT analysis is something that gets easier and better over time. The more experience you have of using this technique, the easier you will find it and the more you will get out of it. My advice, therefore, is to take every opportunity you can to practise your SWOT analysis skills. The beauty of this particular technique is that it can be applied to such a wide variety of situations. There is therefore no shortage of opportunities for practising your SWOT analysis skills.

As a footnote, it is worth noting that Tom Lambert, in his book *Key Management Solutions* (1996b), proposes a variation on the theme of SWOT analysis. He writes about COST analysis with 'C' standing for company concerns, 'O' for opportunity analysis, 'S' for company strengths and 'T' for threat analysis.

Think–feel–do
Taking account of the three dimensions of human behaviour

This is a framework that I used to underpin my *People Skills* book. It is a longstanding, well-established approach to human psychology.

Basically, what it refers to is the idea that any complex human action will involve three dimensions: thoughts, feelings and actions or, to give them their technical terms, the cognitive, affective and behavioural dimensions.

Over the years, I have found this to be a very helpful framework for helping problem solvers to get an overview of the situation. What the technique involves is making sure that we consider all three dimensions in our work. There is no compensation involved here. For example, to concentrate on 'think' and 'feel', and to do so superbly, will not compensate for failure to address the 'do' dimension. It is a bit like a car. An effective car has to have working engine, brakes and steering. The absence of one will not be compensated for by the others. If we are going to do justice to the complexities of the problems we encounter in people work, then we have to make sure that we are covering all three aspects of think–feel–do.

What can often happen is that pressures can lead us to concentrating on those aspects of think–feel–do that we feel most comfortable with. For example, some people feel very comfortable with emotional issues and may concentrate on these at the expense of the other aspects. By contrast, some people may feel uncomfortable in dealing with feelings and will run the risk of not addressing this dimension adequately. We have to be very wary, then, of falling into the trap of sticking more closely to the aspect(s) of this three-dimensional model that we feel most comfortable with and avoiding the aspect(s) we feel least comfortable with. We have to become well-rounded practitioners in this respect, being able to address all three elements.

A pattern I have noticed over the years is for excessive work pressures to have an adverse effect on the use of think–feel–do as a framework. In my experience, the feelings dimension is the most vulnerable. Often, when people become very busy, they can forget to take account of people's feelings (their own and those of other people). You may well have been on the receiving end of this yourself where perhaps, in dealing with somebody from a particular organization, that person is so busy that they fail to take account of your feelings and your needs. This can lead to feelings of anger, thus upping the emotional stakes and perhaps leading to a vicious circle in which the problems escalate.

When pressures get very high, the think dimension can also fail to feature. It means, in effect, that the people concerned are operating on 'automatic pilot'. They are not thinking about what they are doing. They are not thinking about what the appropriate response to their situation is – they are just reacting. This sort of knee-jerk approach is really very dangerous and can have highly detrimental consequences for all concerned.

However, in some extreme circumstances, it is also possible for the 'do' dimension to be neglected. People, in some cases, can become so pressurized that they become paralysed, temporarily at least, by the pressures they face. I have come across examples of people who sit at their desk with a stack of paperwork in front of them but do not feel able to pick up their pen and deal with it. They have become stuck in a very difficult set of circumstances as a result of the pressures they face.

The think–feel–do framework can therefore be a very useful tool for trying to make sure that we are taking account of all three important dimensions and not allowing ourselves to be drawn into focusing on one or two at the expense of the overall picture. What is needed is a well-rounded problem solver to make sure that all three dimensions are being considered.

As with many of the tools presented here, this technique can be used either as a means of self-checking, making sure that we are on the right track, or as a direct tool of intervention. We can actually sit down with somebody who is experiencing problems and talk to them about their thoughts, their feelings and the actions involved (what has happened plus what needs to happen). It can be used as a general tool or specifically in those circumstances where someone is failing to address one of the issues. For example, if somebody is in a very complex situation involving a wide range of feelings, it is understandable that they may concentrate very heavily on the feelings dimension and may need some help to broaden it out to take account of the thoughts and actions that also need to be considered. On the other hand, some people may concentrate in a very pragmatic manner on thoughts and actions and fail to address the emotional dimension, thus running the risk of causing problems for other people (through insensitivity to their feelings, for example) or for themselves by not taking account of the role of their own emotional reactions in the situation.

However this technique is used, it should be borne in mind that it is a tool and much depends on the skills used in putting that tool into use. Think–feel–do can be a very helpful framework, but it needs to be used with skill and sensitivity.

One final note of caution: some people have made the mistake of seeing think–feel–do as a process rather than a framework. They have assumed that think–feel–do should be used in a linear fashion – that is, think then feel then do. This is a misunderstanding and a distortion of the think–feel–do framework. It is not implied within the framework that there should be any order to how these issues are addressed. The point, rather, is to make sure that all three are addressed.

The three Hs

Understanding what motivates people's behaviour

This is a tool that has a lot in common with 'Think–feel–do'. Its basic premise is that our behaviour is governed by three sets of factors, each beginning with the letter H:

- *Head*   Of course, although we are not entirely rational creatures, much of what we do will depend on our thought processes, our reasoning. For example, in deciding to pursue a course of action, much will depend on what I think of the situation, the likely outcomes, and so on. That is, my brain will be engaged in a process of trying to make sense of the situation I am in and deciding the most appropriate way forward.
- *Heart*   As Pascal (1995) put it: 'The heart has its reasons which reason knows nothing of'. Of course, while rational thinking will play a significant part in decision making, emotional factors will also feature. Emotion can play a part in holding us back (fear and anxiety, for example) or in pushing us forward (desire and enthusiasm, for example).
- *Habit*   Despite the strong influence of both head and heart, we must take account of the very powerful influence of habit. Habit is probably one of the most important influences on a person's behaviour. This is largely because habit tends to develop a momentum of its own. That is, if there is nothing to indicate that we should change what we are doing today, then the chances are we will do what we did yesterday – in other words, the habit will continue. The longer it continues, the more established it becomes and the stronger it will be in its influence over us.

The three Hs tool can be used in a number of different ways. It can help us with decision making, for example, and this can apply in terms of our own personal decisions; decisions we make jointly with the people we are trying to help (those whom we are working in partnership with); and in helping groups or teams of people to make decisions. As a decision-making tool it can be very useful in clarifying the factors that are shaping our decision making. We can ask ourselves: 'To what extent is our decision making being influenced by head – that is, rational thought; to what extent by heart – that is, the influence of the emotions; and to what extent habit? A wise decision is likely to be one that takes account of all three of these factors. It will be one that considers carefully the rational side of the decision being made. Are we being logical about this? Are we taking account of the relevant issues? Have we thought it through properly? It will also take account of the emotional dimension of heart. Will this decision motivate or de-motivate people? Will it make them feel good or will it create ill-feeling and resentment? Are we being sufficiently sensitive to emotional issues in making this decision? And, of course, it will also have to address the habit dimension. Are there any strong habits that will scupper this decision? Are there any habits that will support it? Do we have to do any preparatory work in changing or reinforcing habits?

The three Hs can also be used as an analytical tool for understanding complex situations without necessarily being part of a formal decision-making process. The process is very similar to that described above in relation to decision making, but its focus is not so much on making a decision but rather on understanding the complexities of a situation – for example, as part of an assessment. In particular, the three Hs can be useful for exploring people's motivation. What rational thoughts motivate them in a particular direction? What feelings reinforce that motivation? What habits reinforce or block that motivation? In looking at motivation in this way, steps can then be taken to increase motivation in the desired direction or decrease motivation where it is something that we are trying to discourage (an inappropriate or destructive behaviour, for example).

Many people are used to thinking in terms of head and heart or thoughts and feelings and how these affect our behaviour. However, the dimension that is often missing is that of habit. Habit can be seen to apply at two different levels. First of all we have individual habits. Each of us will have a set of habitual behaviours, things that have developed over time that we have become comfortable with. In this respect, habits are very positive. They help to get us through the day. Imagine how difficult it would be to try and get through our lives without having comfortable habits to rely on. However, there is also a downside to habits at this personal level, in so far as we can over-rely on them. We can, for example, adopt a habitual response to an unusual situation and therefore deal with it inappropriately. Too great a reliance on habit can also mean that our creativity and our propensity to work in an innovative way to develop new solutions can be severely limited.

Second, habits can also apply at a broader level and this is usually what we refer to as culture, whether this is a team culture or an organizational culture, or a culture relating to any other collection of people over time. A culture is, in effect, a set of shared assumptions or unwritten rules and this leads to habits forming within that culture. That is, if you are part of a particular culture (say an organizational culture), then it is likely that there will be a certain set of habits associated with this. Think, for example, about your current organizational situation. How would you describe the culture of the organization that you are associated with at present? What are its unwritten rules? What habits are the bread and butter of that culture?

It is important to recognize that habits operate at individual and broader levels. To make sure that, where habits need to change in the spirit of problem solving, then we should not focus just on individual habits, as often collective cultural habits can be much more powerful and also, at times, much more destructive. Some people may feel that the idea of pursuing culture change is overly ambitious. However, it is not a question of changing the whole culture, but rather the more realistic aim of focusing on specific elements – that is, specific habits within that culture that need to be addressed.

One of the lessons that 'Think–feel–do' has taught us is that it is not enough to look at thoughts and feelings without also looking at what has happened and what needs to happen. This lesson should also be applied to the three Hs. While the three Hs can be a very useful decision-making or analytical tool (especially in relation to motivation) we should not lose sight of the fact that actions will need to follow on from our analysis.

Transactional analysis
Understanding interpersonal dynamics

Transactional analysis, or TA as it is commonly known, is a theoretical perspective that is widely used in the caring professions, but can also be used in a management context in any setting. Space does not permit a detailed exposition of it here, so I must limit myself to looking at how one of its basic tenets, ego states, can be helpful in understanding and, where appropriate, changing interpersonal interactions.

According to TA, we can understand how people relate to one another by reference to the interactions of three basic ego states: parent, adult and child. The interactions can take the following forms:

- *Parent–child* If I adopt a parental, authority figure attitude towards you, I am putting you under pressure to adopt a subordinate role – to be a child to my parent. This can also occur the other way round. If you behave in a childish way, not taking responsibility for your actions, then I may well feel the need to adopt a parental mode in order to 'bring you into line'.
- *Parent–parent* If I adopt a parental attitude towards you, and you are not prepared to accept this, then we may enter a power battle in which you try to 'parent' me in return. If we are not careful, this can become very destructive, with both parties adopting childlike attitudes towards the other and to the situation (see child–child below).
- *Adult–adult* This is a good balance to aim for. Each party treats the other with respect and thus creates a sound platform for collaboration and mutual assistance. This does not mean that both parties are necessarily on an equal footing – there may still be significant power differences between the two – but they none the less treat each other with respect. This has much in common with the idea of assertiveness and seeking 'win–win' outcomes.
- *Parent–adult* This too has much in common with assertiveness. In this combination, one person is trying to pressurize the other into a child role, but he or she is refusing to do so, but without falling into the trap of entering a parent–parent conflict situation. The person adopting the adult ego state

remains calm, treats the other person with respect and thus puts him or her under pressure to step down from the parent role to adopt the more reasonable and respectful one of adult.

- *Child–child*   This is where neither party in an interaction is taking responsibility. An example of this I have come across many times is staff working in an environment where they are not happy but, instead of raising the issues through the channels available to them (as adults), they prefer to indulge in gossip and moaning. Constructive (adult) action to make positive changes in an unsatisfactory situation is rejected in favour of potentially destructive 'whingeing'. A little ventilation of ill feelings or resentment can be quite appropriate and helpful, but if it is allowed to dominate, then child–child interactions can become quite corrosive of morale, trust and teamwork (see also the discussion above of 'The drama triangle').

Understanding interpersonal interactions in terms of these various combinations can be quite helpful. It can give us a great deal of insight into what is happening between people. It can help us understand how we are relating to other people and how they are relating to us. Similarly, we can use it to make sense of interactions between others (for example, colleagues or members of a family).

Once we have used the tool to help make sense of the interactions, then we may also be able to use it to try and change those interactions where necessary or where it would be helpful to do so in order to tackle a particular problem or set of problems. Sometimes we may get a very clear message that we need to adjust our own ego state. For example, in working with someone who has a low level of self-esteem and therefore little confidence or assertiveness, we may be drawn into a parental mode. Of course, this could create a vicious circle in which we trap the individual we are trying to help in a cycle of low confidence. That is, if we adopt a parental mode and start 'looking after' them, we are likely to be encouraging a childlike response, which in turn will encourage a further parental reaction on our part. We can be a supportive adult and, in the process, encourage others to be adult, without falling into the trap of being 'parental'.

We may also use this approach to help others adjust their ego states to create more harmonious relationships. However, if we do use it in this way, we will need to be careful about the language we use. For example, some people may be insulted if anyone suggests they are being childlike, while others may feel flattered to be described as 'parental'. We will therefore have to find other, more indirect means of getting the point across.

TA can be helpful in making sense of group or team dynamics. For example, some people may be adopting parent roles while others are playing the child, rather than all aiming to be 'adults'. In some circumstances it can also be used to help change those dynamics, although this is a very skilful and advanced-level task.

Transactional analysis does not have all the answers and should not be overused. However, when used appropriately it can cast a lot of light on relationships. It can provide a good foundation on which we can build our knowledge, skills and experience.

Tuning in
Making connections with the people we are trying to help

———————————

We have already noted that many of the problem situations we are called upon to deal with are characterized by some degree of conflict. Sometimes this is 'real' conflict, in the sense that the interests of the parties concerned are in opposition or at odds with one another. However, it is often the case that the conflict is a *perceived* conflict, in so far as there is no underlying difference of interest, but the perceptions of one or both parties lead to a conflict situation arising. In other circumstances, there is no conflict – real or perceived – but there may be tensions and anxieties that have a similar effect, namely to put barriers between people. It would be very naïve to assume that everybody we are seeking to help will welcome our involvement. Even in those situations where we can be of enormous benefit to someone, he or she may none the less react in a negative and rejecting way, to begin with at least. This may be a defensive reaction on their part because of the pressures and threats involved in the problems they are experiencing, or it may be that they do not understand our role or are suspicious that we have some sort of hidden agenda that could be to their detriment.

In seeking to work with people in a problem-solving way, we must therefore make efforts to ensure that we engage or connect with them in the early stages of the process. This is what is known as 'tuning in'. It generally involves establishing some sort of common ground. This may be on a personal level – for example, establishing that you attended the same school or have an interest in the same sport or hobby, or it may be on a professional level (for example, by clarifying what you both have to gain by working together to resolve the problems being encountered). This can involve clarifying your role in some detail. This is particularly important if your role is one that may not be widely understood. For example, there may be stereotypical assumptions associated with your role that will need to be cleared away for you to have a positive working relationship. Stop for a moment and consider your role. Are there any negative connotations associated with it? For example, if you are a personnel officer, would people possibly assume that you are trying to make them redundant? If you are a social worker, would the stereotype of 'child snatching' stand in the way of good working relations? Even counsellors who generally have no powers to deprive people of their jobs or of their children, may still be viewed with suspicion and mistrust because of the common misguided notion that anyone who needs the help of a counsellor is experiencing psychiatric problems.

How, then, do we 'tune in'? A lot will depend on your interpersonal skills. However, the following pointers should prove helpful:

- *Non-verbal communication*   Are you making appropriate use of body language? For example, are you smiling appropriately? If seated, are you leaning slightly forward to show interest?
- *Time and place*   Have you chosen a venue or a time that may be distracting and thus undermining of your efforts to connect? For example, sitting in a formal office setting may create a degree of formality that acts as a barrier to tuning in.
- *Role and purpose*   Have you clarified your role and the purpose of your involvement? If the individual concerned is unclear about or, worse still, suspicious about your role, this will create further barriers.
- *Pleasantries*   Begin with some small talk to establish a connection. Be careful not to overdo this, as this may make the person nervous. They may feel that you are avoiding getting down to brass tacks, perhaps because you are anxious about giving them bad news. Too much small talk can create these

sorts of fantasies in the mind of the person you are trying to help. However, if you launch straight into the business of the day without some sort of attempt to 'lubricate' the interaction, you may find that you are perceived as being cold and uncaring and, in this way, tuning in will not have worked.

- *Listening* There is no substitute for effective listening. If you want somebody to feel that you are genuinely trying to help them, then it is imperative that you listen, and listen carefully.

This is not an exhaustive list, but you will find that some of the other tools in this part of the book will also be of benefit here – for example, responding to feelings, acknowledging loss and positive strokes.

Although the emphasis has been on how you can use tuning in to work effectively with others, it is also something that you can teach others to do once you feel comfortable with the technique yourself. For example, you may find that there are tensions in a family or in a work group because of this failure of tuning in. Helping people to develop the skills involved in tuning in can be very beneficial in dealing with those problematic situations that involve a breakdown of interpersonal relations or a failure of individuals to develop effective working relations. Sometimes the situations are far more complex than simple tuning in can deal with but, on many an occasion, all that will be required is for one or more individuals to develop the skills of tuning in. Some people do not get past first base because of their lack of skills in this area. For example, on more than one occasion, I have come across managers who have generated considerable resentment within the teams they are supervising because they have not practised skills of tuning in and have simply launched into giving instructions on work-related tasks.

It has to be remembered that problem solving is something that we do *with* people, not *to* them (remember that the P of PRECISE practice refers to 'partnership based'). To be able to help people, we have to be on the same wavelength as them, to a certain degree at least. Establishing that common ground through tuning in is therefore an activity that is well worth practising. The more we do it, the more skilful we can become and the more advanced a level we can practise at, thereby becoming even more effective over time.

Using dissonance
Challenging ingrained views

'Cognitive dissonance' is an important psychological concept. It refers to situations where our brain is telling us that there is a contradiction between two ideas (or 'cognitions'). For example, imagine a situation where you have known somebody for a long time and you have great trust in them. You feel that they would not do anything to harm or betray you, but then imagine that new information comes to light that strongly suggests that this person has acted in a way that is contrary to your interests, that they have let you down in some way or acted against you (for example, spreading rumours about you). In such a situation dissonance is created. That is, there is a lack of congruence between the idea that you can trust this person and the new information that has come to light.

This creates a very uncomfortable feeling that we are not able to tolerate for long. We will want to take some steps to resolve this dissonance. To resolve this dissonance and thus rid ourselves of this very uncomfortable feeling, we will have to either:

1.   abandon our original cognition – that is our idea that this person is trustworthy; or
2.   disregard the new information – 'No, that can't be the case; he/she would not do that to me'.

This is not only a useful concept in helping to explain a great deal of human behaviour in certain circumstances, it can also be used as a technique to create change, particularly attitudinal change. Consider the following dialogue in the context of an investigator dealing with a complaint of sexual discrimination:

Godfrey: I didn't appoint her because I didn't think she was strong enough.
Investigator: Strong in what sense?
Godfrey: In this line of work you have to deal with a lot of difficult and demanding people and I didn't feel that she was up to that.
Investigator: Because she's a woman?
Godfrey: Well, yes, to a certain extent. We all know that men tend to be more robust than women in this sort of thing.

Investigator: In what way?

Godfrey: Men tend to be less intimidated in these difficult circumstances that our staff face.

Investigator: Am I right in thinking that your organization's chief executive is a woman?

Godfrey: Yes, that's right.

Investigator: Is she easily intimidated?

Godfrey: No, certainly not.

Investigator: So, if your chief executive had applied for this post, you would have had no difficulty in appointing her to it? You wouldn't have thought that, as a woman, she would be too easily intimidated?

Godfrey: No.

Investigator: Then how do you know that the particular woman you rejected would have been easily intimidated?

Here, the investigator is making very clever use of cognitive dissonance. He is creating a situation where the assumption that Godfrey is making (that women are too easily intimidated for his purposes) is contradicted by the idea that his organization's chief executive, as a woman, is not easily intimidated. This clever juxtaposition of the contradictory elements will make it more difficult for Godfrey to hold on to his prejudicial assumption about women.

Much of the work a people problem solver gets involved in includes an element of entrenched attitudes that can be obstacles to progress. These may be discriminatory attitudes, as in the example above, or may be self-defeating attitudes, such as a lack of confidence or self-respect. Specifically in relation to the latter case, cognitive dissonance can be put to good use to help raise self-esteem and boost confidence. For example, when someone claims: 'I don't have any skills to draw on', helping them to identify examples of skills they do actually have can create a degree of dissonance that will help to undermine their self-defeating view of themselves as unskilled and therefore incapable.

Using dissonance to create change is a very subtle process. It involves first of all recognizing an attitude or an assumption that is counterproductive or blocking progress, and then skilfully identifying contradictory elements which will create a feeling of dissonance. This needs to be done sensitively, as simply throwing contradictions into the pot in the hope that dissonance will be created is leaving far too much to chance and is therefore a dangerous option. A much safer course of action is to use this technique only where you feel confident that you have been able to identify:

1. the problematic attitude or assumption;
2. an opposing cognition that is likely to create dissonance, and that you are able to put the two together in a way that will not alienate the person concerned and will have a constructive and positive effect.

Interestingly, dissonance can also be used in reverse, as it were. That is, if you encounter a situation where somebody appears to be feeling very uncomfortable, then the concept of cognitive dissonance can be used to try and explore why that is. You can try, for example, to identify whether there are any elements of dissonance in the situation. This can then be used to help the person deal with their uncomfortable feelings. This is particularly helpful in those situations where cognitive dissonance exists, but the individual concerned has not identified the actual contradiction where he or she simply feels uncomfortable, but is confused about the reasons for it. This is not to say that discomfort is always as a result of cognitive dissonance. There can be other causes, but cognitive dissonance is one that is well worth exploring as a possible, if not likely, cause.

Visioning
Developing a vision of the place we want to get to

One of the benefits of 'SWOT analysis' is that it provides a bridge between the present and the future (the top half of the page and the bottom half of the page). It helps us to think about moving forward and, in situations where we are dealing with people and their problems, that is a very important undertaking. This is partly because people experiencing difficulties can often feel as though they are stuck or trapped, and thus not able to make progress or resolve their difficulties. The sense of defeatism and helplessness that can arise from this can be very counterproductive. It is therefore important to have a focus on positive future outcomes.

There are various ways of doing this, but they can all be grouped under the general heading of 'visioning'. What visioning refers to is the ability to foresee a positive future. This approach is often used as part of strategic management – for example, when the question 'where do you expect your organization to be in three years' time?' is asked. However, while this type of visioning clearly is a useful tool for strategic management, it should not be restricted to this domain.

Visioning can be used in a wide variety of situations. What it involves is trying to help people think about how the future might look. One particularly helpful method of doing this, deriving from solution-focused therapy (de Shazer, 1985, 1991), is what is known as 'the miracle question'. In practice situations, the question is phrased in a variety of ways, but in essence, it asks:

> Suppose tonight while you sleep, a miracle happens. When you awake tomorrow morning, what will you see yourself doing, thinking, or believing about yourself that will confirm that a miracle has taken place in your life?

Its aim is to instil a focus on a future minus the problems currently being experienced and thus to begin to develop a positive outlook. Some people may find this difficult to do (particularly anyone who is depressed), but with a little bit of gentle perseverance, support and skilful help, they can be assisted to come up with a vision of the ideal situation. Of course, it is highly unlikely that you will be able to achieve that ideal situation but, by having this vision, it is possible to look at how you can plot a route to get as close to that ideal situation as possible. Also, by identifying the differences between the current situation and the future situation, it is possible to identify what needs to change. This can sometimes be helpful in setting priorities. In some circumstances, there is just so much that needs to change that we can feel overwhelmed by the situation. However, by undertaking this visioning, we can gain an overview that can help us make decisions about which issues to tackle first.

A key element of the solution-focused therapy approach is the need to focus more on solutions than on problems; to try and develop a mindset that focuses on solutions. It is sometimes assumed that, in order to solve a problem, we need to know what has caused it. However, the solution-focused approach challenges this view and argues that, in many circumstances, the solution may have little connection with the cause.

Another approach to visioning is what is known as task-centred practice (Marsh and Doel, 2005). This involves identifying where you are now plus where you want to be and then plotting the route from the former to the latter in terms of the tasks that need to be achieved in order to make progress. An important underlying principle of this approach is that 'nothing succeeds like success'. What this means is that, when beginning to identify tasks that need to be achieved to make progress, we should focus primarily on the easiest tasks in order to boost confidence to give a clear message that progress is possible and to establish a basis of success. Another important principle of task-centred practice is that the tasks that need to be achieved can be shared out – it can be a co-operative effort. Instead of the problem solver simply being an adviser or counsellor, he or she can actively engage in the process by trading off tasks. For example, a problem-solving helper could agree to undertake tasks A, B and C on condition that the person being helped achieves tasks X, Y and Z. Some practitioners take this a step forward by actually producing a written contract – an agreement outlining the goals being aimed for, and the tasks required to achieve them, and who will be responsible for what over what timescale. My own view on this is that it can be very helpful if undertaken skilfully and sensitively. However, if not handled properly, it can simply add an extra layer of bureaucracy and formality that can stand in the way of progress. This is not to rule out the use of written agreements but rather to issue a warning that they need to be handled carefully and sensitively.

Visioning can be used at a range of levels. It can be used as a personal clarification tool. You can sit yourself down and ask yourself where you want to be and how you are going to get there. It can be used as a tool of intervention (as in the example of task-centred practice given above). It can be used as a team development tool for teams to identify where they want to be and how they are going to get there. It can also be used as a strategic planning tool for whole organizations or sub-sections of organizations.

Visioning is recognized as an important part of leadership. It is a skill of established leaders that they are able to identify a vision and work towards achieving it, motivating, or even inspiring, others to share in creating that vision and working towards it. In my view, there is a close link between leadership skills and problem-solving skills. This is because good leaders are often able not only to solve problems that stand in the way of progress towards the identified vision, but may actually, because of their leadership skills, also be in a position to anticipate the problems and 'head them off at the pass'. The other side of the coin is that problem-solving skills in a wide variety of settings, undertaken by people who are not necessarily in leadership positions, may none the less, draw on leadership skills.

Working backwards
Keeping a clear focus on outcomes

This is a technique that has much in common with the idea of visioning discussed earlier. The notion of 'beginning with the end in mind' is one of the seven principles discussed in Stephen Covey's (1992) book *The Seven Habits of Highly Effective People: Powerful Lessons in Personal Change*. What this technique refers to is the idea that, before we go about our business, we should have a fairly clear picture of what we are trying to achieve. In this respect, this technique has much in common not only with visioning but also with systematic practice. As Covey sees it, there are two layers of creation. First, something is created in our minds. Then we have to translate that mental creation into a physical creation. We have to make it happen. There are two key issues involved in this: planning and motivation.

In terms of planning, it is important that we are clear what we are trying to achieve – where we are trying to get to. As the saying has it, if we do not know where we are going, any road will take us there. As we noted in Part One, not having clarity about what we are doing can sap morale and waste a lot of time and energy. The principle of 'begin with the end in mind' is a useful way of keeping this to the forefront of our efforts, trying to make sure that in whatever we do we have clarity about the end product that we are trying to produce.

In terms of motivation, the important thing to recognize here is that it is often our future goals that provide us with motivation. Much of the psychological literature places a great emphasis on the importance of the past (our upbringing, for example) in shaping our present actions and desires. However, it would be a mistake to place too much emphasis on the role of the past and not take account of the role of the future, as part of what motivates us to do what we do today is our desire to be in a different place tomorrow, to achieve particular ends.

The idea of beginning with the end in mind is therefore an important motivational tool. It can be used in two ways. First of all, it is something that we can incorporate into our own actions and thoughts (and in this way is parallel with systematic practice). But we can also use this as a direct technique with the people we are trying to help (either on an individual basis or collectively with groups or teams). We can ask them to work backwards – to 'begin with the end in mind'. This is often referred to as goal setting, the process of identifying specific goals to be achieved. However, goal setting in many quarters has often become a pale imitation of what it should be. It has become a bureaucratic process by which putative goals are identified but, in my experience, it is often the case that these goals rarely drive actual practice in the organization concerned. The connection between the goal and the action is often not maintained. This is where the technique of 'begin with the end in mind' can be helpful. It can help us to move away from the mechanistic process of setting goals for the sake of setting goals and maintain a clear link between the end we are trying to achieve and the actions we need to take to get there.

De Bono (1983) captures the idea of beginning with the end in mind when he describes what he calls 'working backwards':

One of the most powerful problem-solving methods is to work backwards from the hoped-for solution. It is not unlike end-play in chess: 'What preceding state could have led to this position; what pre-preceding states could have led to that state, etc.?' The possible states preceding the solution-state are taken as destinations and we look for states that might have preceded each of them . . . and so on back, until we are within range of where we start. Imagine a car journey from Edinburgh to London. London is the destination so we work backwards from London. 'If only I could get to Hatfield then the journey from there to London is easy. Now I could get to Hatfield easily from Baldock, so now I need to get to Baldock . . .' all the way back to Edinburgh. Although the process is powerful it is by no means easy to use because it requires a very great deal of imagination and conceptual skill. The steps must be small and concrete. It is also necessary to define the desired end-state very clearly. (p. 59)

Two sets of problems are commonly associated with beginning with the end in mind. First, some people may struggle to identify the end they are working towards. This is often a reflection of the problem situation they find themselves in. It may be a very complex and confusing situation, with a lot of pressures and strains. In such circumstances, we should not be surprised to find that many people will struggle to identify the goals they are trying to achieve. Where this occurs, some of the techniques discussed under the heading of visioning can be of value. However, whatever technique we adopt, the important principle to bear in mind is that we must go at his or her pace. There is little point in trying to force somebody into identifying the goal. If this happens, it is likely that, either they will become resistant, thus blocking progress, or they will mechanistically come up with goals to reduce the pressure they are feeling from you. Of course, neither of these is a helpful approach.

Even when we have identified the goals, there may be a problem in coming up with ways of achieving them. This can be for the same reasons: the complexity, the confusion, the pressure, and so on. Here, as a problem-solving helper, we have an important role to play to act as a support through difficult circumstances, to be helpful and constructive, but without taking over. Once we make the mistake of trying to force the issue, we become part of the problem rather than part of the solution. We become an extra pressure for the person concerned to deal with, rather than a support in dealing with the pressures and problems they already face.

In terms of application, working backwards is something that can be used at any time in our attempts to solve people problems. It is something that we should bear in mind at all times as, without this focus on what we are trying to achieve, there is the danger that we will drift away from our purpose, and thus waste time, energy, effort and even money (a risky thing to do in these resource-strapped days). However, there will also be times when this principle is one that is particularly relevant, for example in circumstances where people feel they have lost their way or where they feel stuck and trapped.

PART THREE

Guide to Further Learning

Introduction

In this final part of the book, I present some ideas for follow-up study. The point was made in Part One that the ideas presented in this book draw upon an extensive theory base. While you do not have to be au fait with the theoretical underpinnings before you can use the tools presented in Part Two, I would argue that the deeper your understanding of the ideas on which the tools are based, the better equipped you will be to make best use of the tools. The more informed you are about the theoretical issues, the greater the insight you will have when it comes to using the tools at an advanced level. You should be wary of falling into the trap of seeing practical tools as an alternative to theoretical understanding. As the discussion of reflective practice in Part One confirms, we should be seeking to integrate theory and practice rather than to reject one in favour of the other. The more you understand the theory base linked to the various tools, the stronger a position you will be in, not only to practise at an advanced level, but also to continue learning and developing over time (Thompson, 2000).

Not all of the tools have a literature associated with them, and so this part of the book is organized under themes, rather than in relation to specific tools – although individual tools are mentioned where appropriate. Following the guidelines on further reading, there is a short section which provides details of relevant websites and organizations.

The ideas that inform the discussion about problem solving presented in Part One, combined with the ideas underpinning the specific techniques in Part Two are, as mentioned above, part of a huge theory base that draws on decades of research, theory development and professional experience in psychology, sociology, social work, counselling and management. Drawing specific, detailed links between the guidance provided in this book and the huge theory base on which it draws would be a major undertaking, requiring a book in its own right. What follows, then, is by no means a comprehensive exposition of the underlying theory base but, rather, simply a basic guide to pursuing further study to develop your understanding of the complex issues the book covers.

Further reading

Conflict

Chapter 16 of *People Skills* is a good starting point. Mediation is covered from a family perspective in Lindstein and Meteyard (1996), and from a management perspective in Crawley and Graham (2002). McConnon and McConnon (2004) is also informative. Commercial mediation is discussed in Mackie *et al.* (1995). De Bono (1986) is also well worth looking at.

Elegant challenging is a concept deriving from neuro-linguistic programming (NLP), a topic explored in some detail in Adler (1996), Knight (2002) and O'Connor and Seymour (2003).

Teamwork in specific contexts is covered in Payne (2000) and Onyett (2003), although both contain material that can be helpful in understanding teamwork across a wide range of settings. In addition, see Dearling (2000) which also has wider applicability than its title implies.

Communication

My own book on communication and language (Thompson, 2003b) presents a review of theoretical issues in Part One and then draws out many of the practice implications in Part Two.

Other useful sources include: Rosengren (2000) and Schirato and Yell (2000) which offer good theoretical perspectives, while Hargie *et al.* (2004), Clutterbuck and Hirst (2003) and Turner (2003) offer a management perspective. Guirdham (1999) provides a helpful discussion of communicating across cultures.

Congruence is a concept deriving from NLP – see Adler (1996), Knight (2002) and/or O'Connor and Seymour (2003).

Crisis and change

The basics of crisis intervention are explained in Thompson (1991). Managing change is a topic with a large literature basis. John Kotter is generally recognized as a leading thinker in this field – see Kotter (1996) and (2002).

Change involves loss, which is well covered in Thompson (2002b), a collection of readings about loss and grief. The Introduction is particularly helpful in understanding loss and grief in the context of tackling people problems.

Force-field analysis was introduced in Lewin (1947) and is also explored in Thompson and Bates (1996). (Cognitive) dissonance is a concept arising from the work of Festinger (1957).

Decision making

General texts on this subject include Juniper (1998), and Kourdi (1999). O'Sullivan (1999) is useful in relation to social work.

Making the most of meetings is the subject of Forsyth (1998) and Pincus and Miller (2004).

A classic work in relation to risk assessment is Brearley (1982). See also Moore (1996) and Gigerenzer (2003).

Buzan and Buzan (2003) is an excellent introduction to mind mapping.

Equality and diversity

PCS analysis is discussed in Thompson (2003a) and Thompson (2006). These are also both good introductions to issues in relation to discrimination, equality and diversity. Texts about specific areas of discrimination include: Solomos (2003) on racism; Wilson (2003) on sexism; S. Thompson (2005) on ageism; Swain *et al.* (2004) on disablism; Blasius and Phelan (1997) on heterosexism; and Moss (2005) on religious discrimination.

Managing pressure

The CIA framework is discussed in Thompson (1999). Thompson *et al.* (1994) and Thompson *et al.* (1996) also contain a lot of useful information about pressure and stress. Other texts include: Sutherland and Cooper (2000), Schabracq *et al.* (2001) and, on the legal implications, Earnshaw and Cooper (1996).

Motivation and influencing skills

Adair (1996) is a widely used text on motivation. Influencing skills are discussed in Chapter 14 of Thompson (2002a). See also Lambert (1996a) and Fowler (1998). Negotiation skills are discussed in Godefroy and Robert (1998). REBT is covered in Dryden (1999).

Problem solving (general)

Part Three of *People Skills* covers a range of problem-solving issues under the heading of 'Intervention Skills'. I have found Egan (2002) very helpful, although he does tend to focus on counselling-style interventions for the most part, which does narrow its scope somewhat.

Covey (1992) is a very popular text which contains a lot of useful insights, although its theoretical base is questionable in places due to its reliance on 'biological reductionism' – that is, the tendency to try and explain psychological and sociological factors in biological terms.

If you are approaching people problems from a social work point of view, Thompson (2005) is very good for setting the context of such work.

Lambert (1996b) provides a great deal of food for thought in relation to problem solving for managers, as does Glass (1996).

Relationships

Egan (2002) is again a useful source here. Other helpful texts include: Auhagen and von Salisch (1996) and Duck (1997).

The ability to respond to feelings, or 'emotional intelligence' is covered in Goleman (1996), Merlevede *et al.* (2001) and McBride and Maitland (2002). However, none of these texts does justice to the complexity of emotion, particularly its sociological dimensions. More sophisticated analyses of emotion are to be found in: Bendelow and Williams (1998), Fineman (2000) and Payne and Cooper (2004). A text that is particularly good on gender and emotion is Fischer (2000). Transactional analysis is covered in Berne (1968), a classic text.

The drama triangle is explained in Karpman (1968), downloadable from www.itaa-net.org/TAJNET/articles/karpman01.html

Organizations and websites

The British Association for
   Counselling and Psychotherapy
1 Regent Place, Rugby, CV21 2PJ
T 0870 443 5252
F 0970 443 5160

www.counselling.co.uk

The Chartered Institute of
   Personnel and Development
151 The Broadway, London, SW19 1JQ
T 020 8971 9000
Information and publications relating to workplace issues.

www.cipd.co.uk

MIND
15–19 Broadway, London, E15 4BQ
T 020 8519 2122
F 020 8522 1725
An important mental health organization.

www.mind.org.uk

The Work Foundation
Peter Runge House
3 Carlton House Terrace
London, SW1Y 5DG
T 0870 165 6700
F 0870 165 6701
A source of useful information about workplace issues.

www.theworkfoundation.com

Human Solutions
A site offering free information and advice on a range of workplace
well-being issues.

www.humansolutions.org.uk

References

Adair, J. (1996) *Effective Motivation: How to Get Extraordinary Results from Everyone*, London, Pan.

Adair, J. (1998) *Effective Leadership Skills: How to Develop Leadership Skills*, London, Pan.

Adler, H. (1996) *NLP for Managers: How to Achieve Excellence at Work*, London, Piatkus.

Argyris, C. (1995) 'Action Science and Organisational Learning', *Journal of Management Psychology*, 10(6).

Auhagen, A-E. and von Salisch, M. (eds) (1996) *The Diversity of Human Relationships*, Cambridge, Cambridge University Press.

Bendelow, G. and Williams, S.J. (eds) (1998) *Emotions in Social Life*, London, Routledge.

Berne, E. (1968) *Games People Play: The Psychology of Human Relationships*, Harmondsworth, Penguin.

Blasius, M. and Phelan, S. (eds) (1997) *We Are Everywhere: A Historical Sourcebook of Gay and Lesbian Politics*, London, Routledge.

Bono, E. de (1983) *Atlas of Management Thinking*, Harmondsworth, Penguin.

Bono, E. de (1986) *Conflicts: A Better Way to Resolve Them*, Harmondsworth, Penguin.

Bono, E. de (1990) *Lateral Thinking*, Harmondsworth, Penguin.

Brearley, P. (1982) *Risk and Social Work*, London, Routledge.

Buzan, T. and Buzan, B. (2003) *The Mind Map Book*, London, BBC.

Clarke, M. and Stewart, J. (2003) 'Handling the Wicked Issues', in Reynolds *et al.* (2003).

Clutterbuck, D. and Hirst, S. (2003) *Talking Business: Making Communication Work*, Oxford, Butterworth Heinemann.

Congress, E.P. (2002) 'Using the Culturagram with Culturally Diverse Families', in Roberts and Greene (2002).

Covey, S.R. (1992) *The Seven Habits of Highly Effective People: Powerful Lessons in Personal Change*, London, Simon and Schuster.

Crawley, J. and Graham, K. (2002) *Mediation for Managers: Resolving Conflict and Rebuilding Relationships at Work*, London, Nicholas Brealey.

Dearling, A. (2000) *Effective Use of Teambuilding in Social Welfare Organisations*, Lyme Regis, Russell House Publishing.

Doel, M. and Marsh, P. (1992) *Task-Centred Social Work*, Aldershot, Ashgate.

Drucker, P. (1954) *The Practice of Management*, London, Heinemann.

Dryden, W. (1999) *Rational Emotive Behaviour Counselling in Action*, 2nd edn, London, Sage.

Duck, S. (ed.) (1997) *Handbook of Human Relationships*, London, Sage.

Earnshaw, J. and Cooper, C.L. (1996) *Stress and Employer Liability*, London, Instititute of Personnel and Development.

Egan, G. (1994) *The Skilled Helper: A Problem-Management Approach to Helping*, 5th edn, Pacific Grove, CA, Brooks/Cole.

Egan, G. (2002) *The Skilled Helper: A Problem-Management Approach to Helping*, 7th edn, Pacific Grove, CA, Brooks/Cole.

Ellis, A. (1962) *Reason and Emotion in Psychotherapy*, New York, Lyle Stuart.

Festinger, L. (1957) *A Theory of Cognitive Dissonance*, Stanford, CA, Stanford University Press.

Fineman, S. (ed.) (2000) *Emotion in Organizations*, 2nd edn, London, Sage.

Fischer, A.H. (ed.) (2000) *Gender and Emotion: Social Psychological Perspectives*, Cambridge, Cambridge University Press.

Forsyth, P. (1998) *Making Meetings Work*, London, Chartered Institute of Personnel and Development.

Fowler, A. (1998) *Negotiating, Persuading and Iinfluencing*, London, Chartered Institute of Personnel and Development.

Garfinkel, H. (1967) *Studies in Ethnomethodology*, Englewood Cliffs, NJ, Prentice-Hall.

Gigerenzer, G. (2003) *Reckoning with Risk: Learning to Live with Uncertainty*, Harmondsworth, Penguin.

Gilbert, P. and Thompson, N. (2002) *Supervision and Leadership Skills: A Training Resource*, Wrexham, Learning Curve Publishing.

Glass, N. (1996) *Management Masterclass*, London, Nicholas Brealey.

Godefroy, C.H. and Robert, L. (1998) *The Outstanding Negotiator: How to Develop Your Arguing Power*, London, Piatkus.

Goleman, D. (1996) *Emotional Intelligence: Why it Can Matter More Than IQ*, London, Bloomsbury.

Guirdham, M. (1999) *Communicating Across Cultures*, London, Macmillan – now Palgrave Macmillan.

Hargie, O., Dickson, D. and Tourish, D. (2004) *Communication Skills for Effective Management*, Basingstoke, Palgrave Macmillan.

Janis, I. (1982) *Groupthink: Psychological Studies of Policy Decisions and Fiascoes*, 2nd edn, Boston, MA, Houghton Mifflin.

Juniper, D. (1998) *Making Decisions*, Plymouth, How to Books.

Karpman, S. (1968) 'Fairy Tales and Script Drama Analysis', *Transactional Analysis Bulletin*, 7(26).

Knight, S. (2002) *NLP at Work: The Difference that Makes a Difference in Business*, 2nd edn, London, Nicholas Brealey.

Kotter, J. P. (1996) *Leading Change*, Boston, MA, Harvard Business School Press.

Kotter, J.P. (2002) *The Heart of Change*, Boston, MA, Harvard Business School Press.

Kourdi, J. (1999) *Decision Making*, London, Orion Business Books.

Lambert, T. (1996a) *The Power of Influence: Intensive Influencing Skills at Work*, London, Nicholas Brealey.

Lambert, T. (1996b) *Key Management Solutions*, London, Pitman.

Larrick, R. and Klayman, J. (1998) 'Not Beyond Repair', *FT Mastering Management Review*, December, 1998.

Lewin, K. (1947) 'Feedback Problems of Social Diagnosis and Action', *Human Relations*, 1.

Lindstein, T. and Meteyard, B. (1996) *What Works in Family Mediation: Mediating Residence and Contact Disputes*, Lyme Regis, Russell House Publishing.

Mabey, C. and Iles, P. (eds) (1994) *Managing Learning*, London, Routledge.

Mackie, K., Miles, D. and Marsh, W. (1995) *Commercial Dispute Resolution: An ADR Practice Guide*.

Marsh, P. and Doel, M. (2005) *The Task-Centred Book*, London, Routledge.

Marshall, P. (1998) *Unlocking Your Potential*, Oxford, How To Books.

McBride, P. and Maitland, S. (2002) *EI Advantage: Putting Emotional Intelligence into Practice*, London, McGraw-Hill.

McConnon, S. and McConnon, M. (2004) *Resolving Conflict: How to Manage Disagreements and Develop Trust and Understanding*, 2nd edn, Oxford, How To Books.

Merlevede, P.E., Bridoux, D. and Vandamme, R. (2001) *Seven Steps to Emotional Intelligence*, Carmarthen, Crown House.

Moore, B. (1996) *Risk Assessment: Practitioner's Guide to Predicting Harmful Behaviour*, London, Whiting and Birch.

Morgan, G. (1997) *Images of Organization*, 2nd edn, London, Sage.

Moss, B. (2005) *Religion and Spirituality*, Lyme Regis, Russell House Publishing.

O'Connell, A. (2003) 'The Transfer of Training to the Workplace', *British Journal of Occupational Learning*, 1(2).

O'Connor, J. and Seymour, J. (2003) *Introducing NLP: Psychological Skills for Understanding and Influencing People*, London, HarperCollins.

O'Sullivan, T. (1999) *Making Decisions in Social Work*, London, Macmillan – now Palgrave Macmillan.

Onyett, S. (2003) *Teamworking in Mental Health*, Basingstoke, Palgrave Macmillan.

Pascal, B. (1995) *Pensées*, Harmondsworth, Penguin.

Payne, M. (2000) *Teamwork in Multiprofessional Care*, Basingstoke, Palgrave Macmillan.

Payne, R.L. and Cooper, C.L. (eds) (2004) *Emotions at Work: Theory, Research and Applications for Management*, Chichester, Wiley.

Pincus, M. and Miller, R.F. (2004) *Running a Meeting that Works*, London, Barron's Educational.

Revans, R. (1998) *An ABC of Action Learning*, London, Lemos and Crane.

Reynolds, J., Henderson, J., Seden, J., Charlesworth, J. and Bullman, A. (eds) (2003) *The Managing Care Reader*, London, Routledge.

Roberts, A.R. and Greene, G.J. (eds) (2002) *Social Workers' Desk Reference*, Oxford and New York, Oxford University Press.

Rosengren, K.E. (2000) *Communication: An Introduction*, London, Sage.

Schabracq, M., Cooper, C., Travers, C. and van Haanen, D. (2001) *Occupational Health Psychology: The Challenge of Workplace Stress*, Leicester, BPS Books.

Schirato, T. and Yell, S. (2000) *Communication and Culture: An Introduction*, London, Sage.

Schön, D.F. (1983) *The Reflective Practitioner*, New York, Basic Books.

Scollon, R. and Scollon, S.W. (2001) *Intercultural Communication*, 2nd edn, Oxford, Blackwell.

Senge, P.M. (1994) 'The Leader's New Work: Building Learning Organizations', in Mabey and Iles (1994).

Shazer, S. de (1985) *Keys to Solutions in Brief Therapy*, New York, W.W. Norton.

Shazer, S. de (1991) *Putting Difference to Work*, New York, W.W. Norton.

Solomos, J. (2003) *Race and Racism in Britain*, 3rd edn, Basingstoke, Palgrave Macmillan.

Sutherland, V.J. and Cooper, C.L. (2000) *Strategic Stress Management: An Organizational Approach*, London, Macmillan – now Palgrave Macmillan.

Swain, J., French, S., Barnes, C. and Thomas, C. (eds) (2004) *Disabling Barriers – Enabling Environments*, 2nd edn, London, Sage.

Thomas, W.I. and Znaniecki, F. (1958) *The Polish Peasant in Europe and America*, New York, Dover Publications.

Thompson, N. (1991) *Crisis Intervention Revisited*, Birmingham, Pepar.

Thompson, N. (1995) *Age and Dignity: Working with Older People*, Aldershot, Arena.

Thompson, N. (1999) *Stress Matters*, Birmingham, Pepar.

Thompson, N. (2000) *Theory and Practice in Human Services*, Buckingham, Open University Press.

Thompson, N. (2002a) *People Skills*, 2nd edn, Basingstoke, Palgrave Macmillan.

Thompson, N. (ed.) (2002b) *Loss and Grief: A Guide for Human Services Practitioners*, Basingstoke, Palgrave Macmillan.

Thompson, N. (2003a) *Promoting Equality*, 2nd edn, Basingstoke, Palgrave Macmillan.

Thompson, N. (2003b) *Communication and Language: A Handbook of Theory and Practice*, Basingstoke, Palgrave Macmillan.

Thompson, N. (2005) *Understanding Social Work: Preparing for Practice*, 2nd edn, Basingstoke, Palgrave Macmillan.

Thompson, N. (2006) *Anti-Discriminatory Practice*, 4th edn, Basingstoke, Palgrave Macmillan.

Thompson, N. and Bates, J. (1996) *Learning from Other Disciplines: Lessons from Nurse Education and Management Theory*, Norwich, University of East Anglia Monographs.

Thompson, N., Murphy, M. and Stradling, S. (1994) *Dealing with Stress*, Basingstoke, Macmillan – now Palgrave Macmillan.

Thompson, N., Murphy, M. and Stradling, S. (1996) *Meeting the Stress Challenge*, Lyme Regis, Russell House Publishing.

Thompson, S. (2005) *Age Discrimination*, Lyme Regis, Russell House Publishing.

Turner, P. (2003) *Organisational Communication: The Role of the HR Professional*, London, Chartered Institute of Personnel and Development.

Wilde, J. (2002) *Anger Management in Schools: Alternatives to Student Violence*, 2nd edn, Lanham, Maryland, Scarecrow Press.

Wilson, F.M. (2003) *Organizational Behaviour and Gender*, 2nd edn, Aldershot, Ashgate.

Index